RENAISSANCE DRAMA

New Series XVII ☙ 1986

Renaissance Drama

New Series XVII

Renaissance Drama and Cultural Change

Edited by Mary Beth Rose

Northwestern University Press and

The Newberry Library Center for Renaissance Studies

EVANSTON 1986

Copyright © 1986 by Northwestern University Press
All rights reserved
Library of Congress Catalog Number 67-29872
ISBN 0–8101–0678–7
Printed in the United States of America

Publication of this volume was made possible by a grant from the College of Arts and Sciences, Northwestern University.

200300

Editorial Note

R ENAISSANCE DRAMA, an annual publication, is devoted to understanding the drama as a central feature of Renaissance culture. Coverage, so far as subject matter is concerned, is not restricted to any single geographical area. The chronological limits of the Renaissance are interpreted broadly. Essays are encouraged that explore the relationship of Renaissance dramatic traditions to their precursors and successors; have an interdisciplinary orientation; explore the relationship of the drama to society and history; examine the impact of new forms of interpretation on Renaissance drama; and raise fresh questions about the texts and performances of Renaissance plays.

As of 1986, *Renaissance Drama* has become a cooperative project involving the Newberry Library Center for Renaissance Studies, the English Department at Northwestern University, and Northwestern University Press. This and subsequent volumes will endeavor to continue in the tradition established by Founding Editor S. Schoenbaum and maintained with imagination and skill for the last decade by Professor Leonard Barkan.

Volume XVII is devoted to the topic, "Renaissance Drama and Cultural Change." The seven essays are concerned with the effect that conflict in the social, sexual, political, and religious environment had on the drama. Using a variety of approaches, they also explore the contribution of theatrical forms to the ways in which Renaissance culture was being shaped and changed.

As editor I am very grateful to the members of the Editorial Committee and to Editorial Assistant Frances Dolan. Similar thanks are due to Assistant Editor Janice Feldstein for her diligence and care.

Volume XVIII of *Renaissance Drama* will not be restricted to a single topic or approach. Volume XIX will focus on the texts of Renaissance plays. We are seeking essays concerned with the traditional issues of textual scholarship, as well as essays that explore questions of authenticity and canonization and examine the cultural environment in which the text is created, edited, and produced. The deadline for Volume XIX is October 15, 1987. Manuscripts should be sent with stamped, self-addressed return envelopes.

Renaissance Drama conforms to the stylistic conventions outlined in the *MLA Style Manual.* Scholars preparing manuscripts for submission should refer to this book. Submissions and inquiries regarding future volumes should be addressed to Mary Beth Rose, *Renaissance Drama,* The Newberry Library, 60 West Walton Street, Chicago, Illinois 60610.

Mary Beth Rose
Editor

Contents

vii

RENAISSANCE DRAMA

New Series XVII ❧ 1986

The Old and the New: The Spanish Comedia *and the Resistance to Historical Change*

ANTHONY J. CASCARDI

Fear of the master is indeed the beginning of wisdom.
—Hegel

He who has more obedience than I, masters me.
—Emerson

The major enemy, the strategic adversary is . . . the fascism in us all, in our heads and in our everyday behavior, the fascism that causes us to love power, to desire the very thing that dominates and exploits us.
—Foucault

IN A SERIES of articles which first appeared in print two and three decades ago, historians E. J. Hobsbawm, H. R. Trevor-Roper, Pierre Vilar, and J. H. Elliott advanced the claim that the "modernization" of Europe was precipitated by a variety of circumstances that coalesced in the form of a "general crisis" during the seventeenth century.[1] Despite substantial disagreements among them, their work confirmed the fact that a number of social, political, and economic transformations during this period led to the emergence of capitalist modes of production and exchange and also to the consolidation of the powers of the absolute state.[2] While there may have been manifestations of a nascent capitalism well before the seventeenth century, only at this time did social and economic pressures yield anything like a lasting revolution. Elaborating on Marx's view of the English Renaissance as a transitional stage between the dominance of the feudal aristocracy and that of the commercial bourgeoisie, Hobsbawm, for instance, rec-

1

ognizes that there may have been something at work to unsettle the feudal base of European society as early as the fourteenth century, but concedes that only in the seventeenth was there a full-scale recasting of the socioeconomic order.[3] The notion of "crisis" invoked both by Hobsbawm and by Trevor-Roper is already apparent among writers of the seventeenth century, as is the concept of "decline" which Elliott applies to the case of Spain. Yet if a crisis is thought to indicate "the passage from an ascending conjuncture to one of collapse" (Vilar 60), then it is important to note that the crisis tendencies of the feudal order are seen as being finally *overcome* in the seventeenth century. Thus whatever factors might have continued to resist the newly consolidated modes of production are regarded as in some way limiting or "immobilizing" them. In the case of Spain, for instance, Trevor-Roper points to the survival of the *ancien régime* "as a disastrous, immobile burden on an impoverished nation" (95). And Hobsbawm more generally observes that "Unless certain conditions are present . . . the scope of capitalist expansion will be limited by the prevalence of the feudal structure of society, that is of the predominant rural sector or perhaps by some other structure which 'immobilizes' both the potential labour-force, the potential surplus for productive investment, and the potential demand for capitalistically produced goods, such as the prevalence of tribalism or petty commodity production" (15).

The notion that certain political or social structures may have limited the expansion of capitalism may be useful in accounting for the unevenness of its pan-European development, especially in the seventeenth century, but this still leaves much to be explained about the social and political consequences that early capitalism did have. Why, for instance, did the expansion of the fifteenth and sixteenth centuries not lead directly into an industrial revolution? And why was the emergence of capitalism accompanied by a strengthening of absolutist forms of government? Some provisional answers to these questions have been suggested, respectively, by Maurice Dobb and Perry Anderson. In *Studies in the Development of Capitalism* and in the published debate surrounding that work (see Hilton) Dobb suggests that the embryo of bourgeois productive relations—the accumulation of small pockets of capital and the beginnings of class differentiation within an economy of petty producers—arose within a society that was essentially feudal in its socioeconomic relations. As we shall see in the case of the *comedia,* it is more the caste structure of medieval Spanish society than the economy of feudalism which forms the background of the modernist transformation, but still it is worth noting that the *comedia* appropriates these circumstances for strictly ideological ends, perpetuating premodern modes of awareness at a time when capitalism was elsewhere in Europe firmly afoot. Numerous economic historians have suggested that the Spanish conquests in the New World may have supplied the initial capital necessary for the economic transformation which did indeed take place elsewhere in Europe, but as Perry Anderson rightly notes in *Lineages of the Absolutist State* (61), no other Absolute State in Western Europe remained so resistant to bourgeois development. Thus if classical Marxism frequently comes to grief over the peculiar "lag" that occurs between any transformation in the modes of production and the (ultimately utopian) transformation of social relations, these factors may be seen in the case of Spain to be exaggerated to the degree where it would be more accurate to speak of a *resistance* to modernism than of the simple persistence of medieval values during early modern times.

In reconsidering the phenomenon of modernism in light of the specific case of Spain and in advancing some general notions about the ideological function of the *comedia* during this period, one may begin with the observation that orthodox Marxism has itself been shown to conform to the shape of a literary "comedy" or romance, in which the various ends of secular and sacred narrative—familial harmony, the transcendence of the limiting consciousness of this world—are figured as some social version of the Utopian dream.[4] As we shall see, however, the Spanish *comedia* reinscribes this Utopian vision within the structure of a more complex comedy or romance, so that the Utopian telos serves to occlude an awareness of those same modernizing factors which precipitate the *agon* or "conflict" of each play, the purpose of which may be identified as the effacement of the historical conflict informing the genre as a whole. Thus if Marxism would envision the social changes at work in early modern Europe as in some way instrumental to the ultimate transformation of society, then it would not be unreasonable to read the *comedia* as one of the imaginary (which is to say, ideological) mechanisms through which Spanish soci-

ety was able simultaneously to confront and to resist that transformation. In this sense, the *comedia* may be regarded as a rigorously historical genre, even if that fact is made most evident in its resistance to
historical change: the *comedia* consistently admits a vision of the
"modern" or the "new," yet with equal consistency it sacrifices that
vision in favor of the stability to be achieved through the dominance
of the "old." The Utopian vision which it projects, such as in Lope de
Vega's *Fuenteovejuna,* is drawn explicitly from the past and consists
in the dream of the perpetuation of that past, and its pastoral society,
in the form of a changeless future. Thus a genre which Lope himself
described in the "Arte nuevo de hacer comedias" as exemplary of aesthetic modernism is in practice marshaled in support of the most traditional of value systems, that of honor as measured by *limpieza de
sangre;* the mobile forms of behavior most congenial to capitalism are
limited by rigidly hierarchical social arrangements, ones which leave
little room for the mobility of the self; and the motives which elsewhere in Europe were placed in the service of political, economic, and
philosophical individualism are made subservient to what Ortega y
Gasset described as the "psychology of the masses" and to their virtual
need for domination ("the masses, by definition, neither should nor
can direct their own personal existence, and still less rule society in
general" [11]).[5]

To say this much is already to suggest that the process of modernization in Spain as it passed through the crisis of the seventeenth century
was markedly different from that which occurred elsewhere in Europe. Although it is never legitimate to consider specific ideologies as
the invariable correlates of specific modes of production, one may
grant at least heuristic validity to the proposition that the aesthetic
modernism of the early seventeenth century was an ideological transformation of capitalism and of an emergent "consciousness of class."
Noël Salomon attempted to read the Lopean *comedia* and its glorifica-
tion of peasant existence in terms of the perpetuation of older, feudal
modes of production during such a period ("la société monarcho-
seigneurial de 1600–1640 perpétuait dans les temps modernes . . . un
système de production [placé historiquement entre le système esclava-
giste et le système capitaliste] et tout ce qui en derive" [744–54]). But
the play is for him an expression of genuine peasant insurgency, rather

than the locus of a historical conflict in which the new is met with fierce resistance by the old. While feudalism per se was never as firmly established in Spain as it was in England or France, a social axiology of caste was deeply entrenched. In part for this reason Spain could not easily consolidate a bourgeoisie or readily embrace bourgeois values. In 1600, Martín González de Cellorigo could complain that the middle classes of the fifteenth and early sixteenth centuries had all but vanished. He wrote that "Our Republic has come to be an extreme contrast of rich and poor, and there is no means of adjusting them to one another. Our condition is one in which there are rich who loll at ease or poor who beg, and *we lack people of the middle sort,* whom neither wealth nor poverty prevents from pursuing the rightful kind of business enjoined by natural law."[6] One consequence of this polarization of fortunes was the phenomenon which Pierre Vilar called the "irrationalism" of Spanish society, the paradoxical conjuncture of profligacy and miserliness, of consumption and waste, located within a single class or individual: "The rich man ate, was waited upon, entertained, gave, robbed, and allowed others to rob him. As a result of its situation and predicament . . . Spanish society of 1600, the antithesis of Puritan society, turned its back on saving and investment" (Vilar 60). Both Vilar and J. H. Elliott rightly abjure the notion of a Spanish "temperament" that may have been inhospitable to capitalism; "The Castilians, it is said, lacked that elusive quality known as the 'capitalist spirit.' This was a militant society, imbued with the crusading ideal, accustomed by the *reconquista* and the conquest of America to the quest for glory and booty, and dominated by those very ideals least propitious for the development of capitalism" (Elliott 184). Yet one must somehow account for the fact that Spain made relatively little capitalist use of the same American gold and silver which, in all likelihood, provided the nuclear mass for economic expansion in the rest of Europe during the fifteenth and sixteenth centuries. Elliott points to the steady diversion of capital in Spain toward *censos* (personal loans) and *juros* (government bonds), which carried guaranteed rates of return of between five and ten percent. González de Cellorigo saw in the attraction to these forms of investment debt the same "unproductiveness" that characterized the deployment of land and labor in Spain. Consider the following passage from the *Memorial de la política* (1600):

For when the merchant, lured by the certain profits which the bonds will yield, gives up his business, the artisan his craft, the laborer his field, and the shepherd his flock; when the nobleman sells his lands in order to exchange the amount they are worth for five times that sum in Government bonds, then the real income from their patrimonies will be exhausted, and all the silver will vanish into thin air, at the same time as for his own needs, for those of the lord of the estate, the rentier, the tithe-collector, the tax-farmer and so many others who have some claim to make on the land. Thus, from the bottom of the scale to the top, one may calculate that the ratio of those who work to those who do nothing is of the order of one to thirty. . . . Wealth has not taken root because it has remained, and still does remain, etherealized in the form of papers, con-tracts, bonds, letters of exchange and gold or silver coinage, and not in the form of goods able to bear fruit and to attract wealth from abroad by virtue of the wealth within.[7]

On the subject of *censos* and *juros* and the lethargic climate of cap-ital investment in Spain, Cellorigo and others did not go completely unheard. In 1617 the Council of Finance complained that there was no chance of a Castilian economic revival as long as the bonds offered better rates of return than could be gained from investment in agricul-ture, industry, or trade.[8] Thus the apparent "failure" of capitalism in Spain might better be explained as the resistance to capitalism and to the more encompassing "modernization" of society that threatened to displace the fierce traditionalism of the Middle Ages and early Renais-sance. While the contrast between Spain and the rest of Europe cannot be limited to these terms, still it is instructive to compare the most ex-treme manifestation of this traditionalism, the Spanish structure of so-cial castes, with the class structure prevalent in the rest of Europe and North America. Because a caste society forms its evaluations primarily along racial lines and construes value in connection with lineage rath-er than personal wealth, there is little or no incentive to deploy eco-nomic capital toward the increase of value as a means to improve so-cial standing; indeed, the very notions of profit or the increase of value are alien to the axiology of caste.[9] A caste society is overtly mor-al in its evaluations, but only covertly economic.[10] And because caste divisions are racially drawn, they produce a hierarchy that is relatively "closed," especially when compared with the mobility that is in prin-ciple open to members of a class society.[11] This fact remains true even where one takes the notion of "caste" in its weaker form, as José Antonio Maravall does, as indicating a structure of inherited offices and professions.[12] Still, the consequences of such an arrangement are a social sedimentation in which status and the value accorded to professional functions are rigidly circumscribed. The "traditional" order of society thus preserved, which Maravall perceives to be "medieval," is nearly identical to that which is put forward in neo-Scholastic terms by Calderón in his theological *comedias* and *autos sacramentales.* Consider especially the ways in which the apportionment of social roles into castelike divisions is seen as sanctioned either by nature or by God:

Traditional society was founded on the idea that each person had a fixed and determined social function; that a definite social position corresponded to that function; that this carried with it a natural and proper mode of behavior for the possession and enjoyment of economic goods, whose limits were not to be transgressed; that all this was determined by known procedures, and that in accordance with such circumstances, unchangeable in themselves, there belonged to each one a certain education and cultural heritage. . . . As the external projection of this conjuncture of personal facts, identifiable with a place in the fixed social order [*un emplazamiento estamental*], each one was to use his resources and to present himself before others in such a way that his place in the social hierarchy could be recognized immediately. (Maravall, *Teatro y literatura* 41–42)

Ever since Américo Castro published his reinterpretation of the notion of "honor" in the Golden Age in *De la edad conflictiva,*[13] it has been apparent that the Spanish *comedia* was in some special way indebted to the axiology of caste. In the strongest formulation which Castro offered, the preoccupation over honor in view of potential threats to the bloodline provided the theater of Lope de Vega and his successors with its very reason for being ("La presencia del motivo de la honra en el teatro de Lope de Vega y la razón de existir aquel teatro son dos aspectos de una misma conciencia colectiva," *De la edad conflictiva* 49); as Lope himself remarked in the "Arte Nuevo," honor plots were able forcefully to move every member of the audience to enter into the sufferings of the stage heroes ("Los casos de la honra son mejores, / porque mueven con fuerza a toda gente" [327–28]). Yet Castro never considered the possibility that the axiology of caste might have served an ideological function, that this structure of social relations might have continued to emit "signals" (of which the *comedia* would have been one) long after the period of its historical efficacy was past. And yet this is precisely the possibility which must be considered in view of the fact that during the time of the *comedia*'s greatest prestige, in roughly the period from 1580 until Calderón's death a hundred years later, the three racial castes of Spain were reduced to one, thus placing in jeopardy the very structure on which the Spanish "traditionalism" of the Middle Ages was founded.

I have suggested that the axiology of caste may have taken on an ideological function in the *comedia,* but it is not so much Castro's extension of the idea of caste beyond its proper historical bounds which is the target of this critique as Maravall's simplistic analysis of the ideological structure of the genre. On his reading, the "traditional" order of society envisioned by the Spanish drama is one which was imposed on it in the interests of maintaining the status quo, in much the same way, and through many of the same techniques, that a theology was "imposed" by the preachers and moralists of the Baroque.[14] In Maravall's judgment, Spaniards made use of the *comedia* in order to legitimize a structure of social relations founded on the practical domination of one group by another and, in so doing, to avoid the ethical questions which such situations of domination are bound to raise ("Los españoles emplearon el teatro para, sirviéndose de instrumento popularmente tan eficaz, contribuir a socializar un sistema de convenciones, sobre las cuales en ese momento se estimó había de verse apoyado el orden social concreto vigente en el país, orden que había que conservar, en cualquier paso, sin plantear la cuestión de un posible contenido ético," *Teatro y literatura* 32–33). Yet nearly the reverse would seem to be closer to the truth. As we shall see exemplified in *Fuenteovejuna,* it is precisely an ethical opposition, that of absolute good and evil, which organizes the ideological "content" of the *comedia.* Ethics serves for the advancement of an ideology in such a way that the perfect closure offered by the binary oppositions of good and evil, right and wrong, self and other, function as what Fredric Jameson has called "strategies of containment,"[15] in this case as strategies for the containment of the modernizing threats to the traditional caste structure of Spanish society.

One may well be surprised to discover a strategic conservatism in the *comedia,* especially in light of the fact that the poetics of the genre, as conceived and articulated by Lope de Vega, are uniformly modernizing. Lope's "Arte nuevo de hacer comedias" seeks to locate the *comedia* in the very vanguard of artistic practice; even in the title, the emphasis falls on what Lope considers to be the "*new* way of writing plays." As is common among vanguard aesthetics, and notwithstanding the fact that the "Arte nuevo" was commissioned by a Madrid Academy, Lope's stance is explicitly anti-academic. In characteristically modernist fashion, Lope speaks of his as a practice which is not simply innovative but wholly discontinuous with the recognized traditions:

> cuando he de escribir una comedia,
> encierro los preceptos con seis llaves;
> saco a Terencio y Plauto de mi estudio,
> para que no me den voces.
>
> (40–43)

(when I must write a play, I lock up the rules with six keys; I throw Terence and Plautus out of my study so that they won't scold me.)

> Mas ninguno de todos llamar puedo
> más bárbaro que yo, pues contra el arte
> me atrevo a dar preceptos, y me dejo
> llevar de la vulgar corriente, adonde
> me llamen ignorante Italia y Francia.
>
> (362–66)

(But I can call none of these [writers] ruder than I, since I dare to give precepts that contravene the rules, and I allow myself to be carried by the common stream, where Italy and France may call me ignorant.)

In terms of aesthetic practice, however, the *comedia* roundly contradicts the modernizing claims made for it in the "Arte nuevo." Whereas Lope argues for the discontinuity of the *comedia* from known traditions, the configuration of the genre in fact depends on the formation of highly visible internal continuities. These are generated in part from its sources in the chronicle and ballad traditions and accordingly issue in structures which are more narrative than dramatic. Thus Lope can refer to the elements of the *comedia* as the parts of a generic narrative formula which, in theory at least, are capable of infinite repetition (e.g., "divide the subject in two parts, establish the connection from the beginning"; "place the problem in Act One, tie the events together in Act Two" [231–32, 298–99]). The regulation of subject matter and form similarly becomes a question of the interchange of nearly preprogrammed units (e.g., "*Décimas* are good for complaints; / the sonnet works well for those who wait; / stories must be told in ballad-verse," 307–09).[16] In practice, Lope's aesthetic of continuity requires a grace and an elegance which presuppose the natural equivalence of style and form:

> Si hablare el rey, imite cuanto pueda
> la gravedad real; si el viejo hablare,
> procure una modestia sentenciosa.
>
> (269–71)

(If a king should speak, let him imitate insofar as possible the seriousness of a king; if an old man should speak, strive for an unassuming pithiness.)

> Remátense las scenas con sentencia,
> con donaire, con versos elegantes,
> de suerte que, al entrarse el que recita,
> no deje con disgusto el auditorio
>
> (294–97)

(Finish off the scenes with wit and grace, with elegant verses, so that when someone comes onstage to speak, he will not leave the audience displeased.)

In pleading for the autonomy of the *comedia* from any recognized rules, Lope goes considerably beyond the notion of artistic convention that was characteristic of the European neoclassical traditions of the sixteenth and seventeenth centuries.[17] He argues from a notion of taste (*gusto*) which is revealingly indicative of the commodification of the aesthetic object and of the ideological functions which any commodity may serve. Taste, as Lope understands it, refers principally to the preferences of the paying public (Pierre Vilar remarked that the *comedia* was in fact the only literary genre which "paid its way" in Golden Age Spain [70]); yet by virtue of its mass appeal the *comedia* was able to create in the public the very desires which it was designed to satisfy: "como las paga el vulgo, es justo / hablarle en necio para darle gusto" (47–48), a passage which I would render in the following strong translation: "since the common people pay for these plays, it is right to speak to them like fools in order to please them." Thus if the *comedia* can be seen to enact a conflict between tradition and modernity, caste and class, old and new, this is accomplished in such a way that the pressures of the modern are consistently masked; the fundamental conservatism of the genre acquires all the force of an ideology which is welcomed by the masses and willingly taken on by them.

The dramatic energies thus generated may be made immediately apparent if one considers for a moment the case of Tirso de Molina's *El Burlador de Sevilla.* On one level, the figure of Don Juan would appear to be the very antithesis of the scheme that I have proposed thus far: if the *comedia* sustains a traditional and conservative ideology through the establishment of continuities, then Don Juan is both modern and subversive. His principal effort is to come into contact with a reserve of psychosexual energy which he discharges in the form of discontinuous flows. The fragmentary nature of his experience is marked by his rapid flight after each amorous conquest ("¡Ensilla, Catalinón!" ["Saddle up, Catalinón!"]), and since he makes no connection between one experience and the next the very structure of the play may be read as an attempt to subvert even the narrative continuities on which the *comedia*'s conservative ideology rests. As the inversion of the prototypical *comedia* hero—the hero who sustains his identity through an inflexible allegiance to the idealist principles of selfhood and honor ("Soy quien soy" ["I am who I am"])—Don Juan is able to join Shakespeare's Iago and those who subversively are able to fashion an identity from its near-demonic displacement through a series of disguises and feints (Iago: "I am not I"; Don Juan: "Soy un hombre sin nombre" ["I am a nameless man"]). Insofar as Don Juan thus attempts to free himself from the social structuration of power, he may fairly be described as the subversive or revolutionary characterized by Gilles Deleuze and Felix Guattari. The essential task of the revolutionary, as outlined in *L'Anti-Oedipe,* is "to learn from the psychic flow how to shake off the Oedipal yoke and the effects of power, in order to initiate a radical politics of *desire freed from all beliefs.* Such a politics dissolves the mystifications of power through the kindling, on all levels, of antioedipal forces—the schizzes-flows—forces that escape coding, scramble all the codes, and flee in all directions: orphans (no daddy-

mommy-me), atheists (no beliefs), and nomads (no habits, no
territories)."[18] As an anti-narrative, *El Burlador de Sevilla* threatens to
dissolve into the simply repetitious and potentially gratuitous actions
of Don Juan. And yet Tirso encloses this anti-narrative within a frame-
work that, by virtue of the telos of divine justice and punishment, sub-
sumes Don Juan within the most orthodox of theocentric paradigms.
In this way, it may be said that the ideological consciousness most revealingly exposed in *El Burlador* corresponds not to that of Don Juan
but to the women whom he conquers: theirs is a consciousness not of
the colonizer but of the colonized, a consciousness not simply of desire but of the desire for conquest and domination.

Let us return, however, to the terms suggested by Lope de Vega in
the "Arte nuevo." To view the *comedia* as one of the first truly com-
modified aesthetic objects is in the first instance to regard it as a practice fully located in history, where "history" is determined primarily
as the relationship among those elements of a culture which Raymond
Williams called "dominant," "residual," and "emergent" (121–27). A
play like *Fuenteovejuna* takes as its subject the conflicts between the
aristomilitary caste (the Comendador of the Order of Calatrava) and
the peasants (the townspeople of Fuenteovejuna), which resulted in a
civil uprising and the murder of the Comendador in 1476. Yet the historical dimension of the work is apparent only in view of the value
which Lope de Vega, writing during the "critical" years of the seventeenth century, ascribes to these events. The historical "crisis" of the
seventeenth century was produced by the clash of an emergent (modernist) culture with the culture of dominance, yet Lope "translates"
this crisis into the late fifteenth century (a distinctly premodern period) and draws on the archaic resources of Platonic idealism and myth
in order to contain that crisis within acceptable bounds.[19] To subsume
the Utopian tendencies of *Fuenteovejuna* and similar works within a
historical paradigm is thus to reverse the Platonizing interpretations
which have been put forward in the leading formalist and stylistic interpretations of the genre (those of Leo Spitzer, Joaquín Casalduero,
Karl Vossler, Alexander Parker, William McCrary, and Bruce Wardropper), all of which are to some degree totalizing in intent and all of
which may be seen to repress their own historicity by framing their
perspectives so as to preclude any engagement of the concept of ide-

ology or the possibility of a political *non dit*. If one considers Spitzer's reading of *Fuenteovejuna* as a paradigmatic example of this type of criticism, it becomes apparent that such an approach not only de-historicizes the play but, in so doing, unwittingly absorbs the ideological conservatism which the work advances. Spitzer reads *Fuenteovejuna* as the fulfillment of a dream of universal harmony, "the naive dream of a Christian World Harmony, cherished by the Spanish poet of the Golden Age Lope de Vega."[20] His image of the village is of a place of beauty and innocence, outside of history, and his notion of Lope's accomplishment is that of having preserved an Arcadian or Utopian existence by the transcendence of history. Applauding Casalduero, who he says was the first to demonstrate that the play has "no political or revolutionary purpose . . . but treats a metaphysical or moral problem,"[21] yet faced with the fact that *Fuenteovejuna* has a manifest political content, Spitzer ascribes politics to the forces of some demonic agency, to "transient and dark forces of disorder":

Lope worked, as it were, from the historical battle-cries, backward to their metaphysical source. By means of this projection he was able to lift the original village of Fuenteovejuna out of time and space as an island of metaphysical peace, the realization of the Golden Age in the midst of our age of iron, the locus of cosmic harmony in the midst of our world of chaos, at the same time an Arcadia and a Utopia. Thus the "political action" to which the villagers are forced to resort (and with which the drama is mainly concerned) is due only to a temporary and local invasion of that idyllic, timeless peace that is the principle of *any* "Fuenteovejuna," by transient and dark forces of disorder. (209)

In Spitzer's and Casalduero's approach, the concrete historical conflict between the Comendador and the town is seen as the defect or "lack" of perfect relations—where the standards of perfection are identical to those which Nature provides—rather than as structurally a part of the relationship between unequal groups, dividing those who defend and rule from those who work. Accordingly, the actions of the Comendador are abjured for the "irresponsibility" which they demonstrate toward the town, where the notion of responsibility is understood in strictly idealist terms. It is often said in this regard that as feudal lord of the town the Comendador should be responsible for the well-being of his vassals, and that he fails in his duty. What, then, is one to say of the fact that this "failure" takes the exceedingly violent form of sexual aggression? Similarly, as Comendador of Calatrava he is under obligation to protect the Crown, yet he enlists the support of the Master of the Order in a plot for the capture of Ciudad Real, the ultimate implication of which is political treason. Even where such a reading does acknowledge the historical conflicts which form the ostensible subject of the play, history is seen primarily as the object of moralizing critique. The Comendador's actions are taken as symptomatic of a certain malaise, the decadence of the Military Orders whose purpose was originally the defense of Christendom against Islam:

> la cruz roja obliga
> cuantos al pecho la tienen
> aunque sea de orden sacro;
> mas contra moros se entiende

(the red cross imposes an obligation on all who wear it on their chest, even though it is [the sign of] a holy order; but one means fighting against Moors.)

In spite of Spitzer's thoroughgoing Platonism—or perhaps *because* of it—his reading of *Fuenteovejuna* serves to make plain the fact that this *comedia* conforms to the shape of literary romance, which Arnold Reichenberger saw as characteristic of the *comedia* as a genre (307). The *comedia* moves, in Reichenberger's words, from "order disturbed to order restored," or in structural terms from *agon* to utopian resolution. The historical and political conflicts which comprise the *agon* of romance are characteristically set in what has been called the "mid-world," and also in the middle of the action, while there is at the same time a strongly teleological pull toward narrative and social closure: the telos is imagined in the form of a future which resists historical change. If Fuenteovejuna is an example of uncorrupted Nature, of the *locus amoenus,* then the Comendador may on one level be identified as the antagonist who disrupts that idyllic harmony, precipitating a nearly mythical "fall" from a state of innocence and grace, in whose wake there follows the rapid degeneration of all that may be called "natural": the labors of the peasants, ordered in accordance with the cycles of nature, are violently disrupted, and social relations begin a process of corruption by division; by the beginning of Act 3, the town has been split from its leader, the women are divided against the men, and the lovers Laurencia and Frondoso are separated from one another. Indeed, nature itself begins to show signs of decadence, and there are auguries of a poor harvest for the coming year ("el año apunta mal, y el tiempo crece, / y es mejor que el sustento esté en depósito" ["The harvest augurs badly and the year is wearing on; it is best that we have some food in storage"]).

Even if the notion of romance as described above is able to accommodate a vision of the Comendador as an agent of historical change, Spitzer's reading is nonetheless guided by the same principle that Fredric Jameson saw in Northrop Frye's archetypal approach to romance: "his identification of mythic patterns in modern texts aims at reinforcing our sense of the affinity between the cultural present of capitalism and the distinct mythical past of tribal societies, and at awakening a sense of the continuity between our psychic life and that of primitive peoples" (130). For Spitzer and those critics of the *comedia* who follow him, this principle of historical identity works by the machinery of transcendence: the decadence which mars the idyllic existence of *Fuenteovejuna* can reasonably be overcome, and the Utopia which Lope projects is in principle accessible to any historical community— including our own—if only it can sufficiently purify its collective life.

If romance lends itself to this style of moralizing critique, this is because the oppositions which organize it may be reduced to a pair that is itself essentially ethical in nature, the struggle of good and evil. As Nietzsche showed in *The Genealogy of Morals, Beyond Good and Evil,* and the fragments assembled as *The Will to Power,* however, the concepts of ethics of the kind we have seen to govern a romance like *Fuenteovejuna* are themselves the sedimented remains of the concrete praxis of situations of domination. Nietzsche demonstrated that what is meant by "good," for instance, is nothing more than my position as an unassailable center of power, in terms of which the position of anyone who is radically different from me (e.g., the weak) is marginalized as an "other" whose practices are then formalized in the concept of "evil." The Christian "reversal" of these circumstances, which we apparently witness in *Fuenteovejuna*, the revolt of the weak against the strong, and the generation of the repressive ideals of charity, care, and self-denial, are no less a function of the initial power structure than are the "ideals" of which they are supposedly the inversion.[22] Consider in this light the closing words of Esteban and the King in *Fuenteovejuna;* the laborers willfully submit themselves to the authority of an absolute monarch, while the King looks forward to the time when he can appoint a new feudal lord:

ESTEBAN
Señor, tuyos ser queremos.
Rey nuestro eres natural.
. . . .
REY
Y la villa es bien se quede
en mí, pues de mí se vale,
hasta ver si acaso sale
comendador que la herede.

(III. 2436–37, 2449–50)

(*Esteban.* Sir, we wish to become your own. You are our natural king. *King.* It is right for the village to remain as mine, since I am responsible for it, until such time as there may be a comendador to inherit it.)

Despite the strong tendency of the *comedia* to achieve narrative and social closure, moments such as these reveal the fact that such closure is achieved only by the erasure of power relations, or by what one recent critic has called the process of "euphemization." And yet what is effaced or repressed invariably returns, most often in the form of a repetition. Consider the prospect alluded to in the passage above, of Fuenteovejuna once again under the domination of a feudal lord; or consider the fact which has long puzzled critics about Calderón's ritualistically brutal *El médico de su honra,* namely, that Gutierre insists before the King that he may find his second wife unfaithful and that he may kill her as he killed the first. As if to remind us of the remainders of power which will not be erased, even in a genre which strives so hard to achieve perfect closure (e.g., the marriage of couples, the justice of God or of the King), there is at the end of *El médico* a bloody hand on Gutierre's door, and this blood will not wash off.

If Nietzsche's "deconstruction" of the ethical binary can be taken to apply to the *comedia* qua romance, then what remains is to ascribe specific values to the "concrete situations of ethical domination," in order to avoid reinscribing the *comedia* back into the idealizing structures from which we have been unable to clear free. A properly historicized reading of *Fuenteovejuna* would begin from the struggles represented in it—the mythical and historical conflicts between Fuenteovejuna and the Comendador, between the Order of Calatrava and Ciudad Real, and ultimately between the Catholic Monarchs of Spain and Alfonso V of Portugal—and proceed from there to an investigation of the motives at work behind the play's romantic and utopian passions. In this way, *Fuenteovejuna* as a structured whole can be seen as determined by the historical "crisis" outlined above, viz., the exhaustion of one socioeconomic order at a time when the newly emerging order is met with resistance and, perhaps, with fear. It is because of this resistance to change that *Fuenteovejuna* and the *comedias* it most resembles can project a future which is fundamentally identical with the past, one in which the tradition-oriented system of racial castes and inherited professions, of "natural" social and political relations, is protected from the reifying effects of the universalization of equivalent labor-power and from the free circulation of capital which the market system would abet. And insofar as the *comedia* may be seen as a strategy for the *containment* of these modernizing forms of existence and their ideological correlates, the genre may be described as the locus of a struggle between that traditional axiology which drew strength from the persistence in Spain of a system of racial castes, and the more modernizing ideology of social class.

If one historicizes romance in this way and views the narrative dis-. position of its elements in terms of the ideologies encoded by them, then the manifest structural and thematics of a play like *Fuenteovejuna* (e.g., of Comendador and town, of self-love and altruism, of *amour propre* and the general will) would have to be rewritten as the elemental constituents of a more essential romance, the principal condition of whose figuration is the historical one mentioned above, i.e., a moment of crisis or transition in which two competing modes of production, or stages of socioeconomic awareness, uneasily coexist as "dominant" and "emergent" portions of a cultural discourse. If this is so, then the Comendador would seem to function neither as the antagonist of romance, whose behavior is monstrously, and predictably, evil, nor as the demonic agent of history who disturbs Fuenteovejuna from the slumbers of its collective life and disrupts the idyll of its natural existence. Insofar as his relations with the town are determined according to a scale of quantitative pleasures and use-value, he is more accurately the decadent member of a caste society whose deeply historical resentment is manifested in the form of sexual and political acquisitiveness.[23] The crucial point of his opposition to the town would then lie in the fact that their relations with one another are determined according to qualitative standards, and their relationship to the products of their labor seen in strictly essentialist terms (cf. Edward M. Wilson's confirming judgment that in the relationship between Casilda and Peribáñez, "The husband [sees] in Casilda the fruits of the earth which he cultivates" [134]).

To the extent that the *comedia* may be seen as a struggle not simply of ethical or metaphysical forces but of different moments of socioeconomic awareness, it demonstrates marked affinities with the ideology of romance as described by Jameson in his essay on the dialectical use of genre criticism ("Magical Narratives"). Yet when one assigns specific values to the modes of socioeconomic consciousness which actually do come into conflict in it, then it becomes clear that the *comedia* significantly modifies the historical terms of Western romance as outlined in that essay. On Jameson's account, the binary oppositions which form the manifest content of romance are characteristic of those periods of history sometimes designated as "times of trouble," times more accurately associated with the degenerate phases of epic society such as one might see reflected in Guillén de Castro's *Las mocedades del Cid,* or with the archaic forms of social movement studied by Hobsbawm in *Primitive Rebels*—times when, in Jameson's words, "central authority disappears and marauding bands of robbers and brigands range geographical immensities with impunity" (118).[24] Romance of the "second-order" type he is discussing is seen as the historical engagement of that conflict which ensues when the rigidly binary mode of thinking characteristic of such times is confronted by the consciousness of a group which has overcome its social and geographical isolation and has developed an awareness of itself as a universal "subject" of history. Romance would provide a means of "solving" the problem of that group's need for (political) recognition and the legitimization of its power by subordinating the consciousness of another to its own. The result is a "new kind of narrative, the 'story' of something like a semic evaporation. The hostile knight, his identity unknown, exudes that insolence which marks a fundamental *refusal of recognition* and stamps him as the bearer of the category of evil, up to the moment when, defeated and unmasked, he asks for mercy by *telling his name*" (Hobsbawm 4; first italics mine). Yet insofar as *Fuenteovejuna,* and the Spanish *comedia* in general, resists the emergence of anything resembling a "consciousness of class," it seeks to dissolve these and similar power relationships into a neutral, not to say natural, hierarchy. The demonic agent in Fuenteovejuna is eliminated rather than reassimilated into the social order, as would be the case according to the paradigm Jameson proposes; in this way the King can call the people of the town his "proper" vassals and can place himself above them, but in a hierarchy which is neutralized insofar as he is seen as their natural ruler (e.g., "Y la villa es bien se quede en mí"; "Rey nuestro eres natural"). To say that the ideological content of romance turns on the problem of recognition (or the refusal thereof) is to imply that romance is deeply political, even if the politics which it advances depends, as in the case of the *comedia,* on the effacement of modern "subjectivity" or class consciousness. The action of *Fuenteovejuna* consists largely in the formation of a political consciousness out of passion and self-interest, yet the political is marked by a peculiarly utopian conjuncture. Similarly, the resolution of the plot may indeed depend on the pronouncement of a name, but this does not give the identity of a "bearer of evil" (i.e., one whose recognition is refused outright); rather, it names the group whose admission of collective responsibility ("Join the town together in one voice"; "Fuenteovejuna killed the Comendador," vv. 1801, 2107) is meant to negate the self-arrogating will of the Comendador, the proudly named Fernán Gómez de Guzmán.

Accordingly, one must seek a model for the political struggle for recognition in the *comedia* which would allow for the fact that independence and acknowledgment in it are granted not to those who defend and rule but to those who work and serve. To the extent that the *comedia* translates this struggle for political recognition into the Platonic terms that Spitzer and Casalduero saw in *Fuenteovejuna,* it asks to be read as analogous to the Hegelian text on which Marx was eventually to perform his materialist operation. The caveat which must be entered is that in the case of the *comedia* the struggle which most nearly prefigures the social transformation which Marx foresaw, the dialectic of Master and Slave, here takes the form of a *huis clos,* a dialectic with no exit. In Hegel's account of the conflict of bondsman and lord, these twin aspects of consciousness are seen as radically unequal and fiercely opposed: the one is independent consciousness, whose nature is to be "for itself" (the Comendadores of *Fuenteovejuna* or *Peribáñez* and, perhaps, the King as well), while the other is dependent consciousness (the villagers, Peribáñez) whose essence is to live "for another." As part of the embracing project of consciousness to achieve independence, each seeks the recognition of the other; and since each must be willing to stake his own life on this pursuit, the dialectic of their relationship naturally proceeds through a trial by death: "it is only through staking one's life that freedom is won. . . . The individual who has not risked his life may well be recognized as a *person,* but he has not attained the truth of this recognition as an independent self-consciousness. Similarly, just as each stakes his own life, so each must seek the other's death, for it values the other no more than itself" (*Phenomenology* 187). The outcome of the struggle of master and slave is recognition but, as Hegel says, "a recognition that is one-sided and unequal" (191). Both are, moreover, deeply unsatisfied: the slave remains dependent, and the lord achieves recognition from a consciousness that is dependent on, and not independent from, his own. Thus it may be said that "the truth of the independent consciousness is the servile consciousness of the bondsman" (193) or, in more strictly Marxist terms, that "the truth of ruling-class consciousness (that is, of hegemonic ideology and cultural production) is to be found in working-class consciousness" (Jameson 290).

The conflict of master and slave which takes place within consciousness is a mythical representation of the historical process by which the self seeks to achieve independence in its relations with others. Not least because of its radical instability, it is a conflict which brings us to the very edge of historical time and to the war and the work of self-consciousness contained within history, properly speaking. Thus the *comedia* as seen from the dialectic of master and slave may be regarded as the effort to educate the slave in the enjoyment of his servile condition, which is to say, in deriving pleasure from his work.[25] Thus while the powerful struggle for acknowledgment and independence of masters and slaves is reduplicated within history, the unhappiness generated therefrom is not entirely unmitigated; even the "unhappy consciousness" is not altogether unhappy: the *comedia* proceeds toward a nearly obligatory "happy ending"; the slave will know moments of enjoyment, despite his subservience to the master, and may indeed come to find satisfaction in the self-alienating nature of his work.

Consider *Peribáñez* in this light. The play has been seen as moving from a state of inauthentic or "false" consciousness on the part of *Peribáñez* to a state of self-awareness. In the judgment of one recent critic, this process begins in Peribáñez's "loss" of self-awareness, a loss signaled most notably by his acceptance from the Comendador of certain gifts, including a set of expensive wall-hangings embroidered with the Comendador's coat of arms (Larson 67–68). Yet the conclusion of the play may be seen to lie not in the recovery of an "authentic" self-consciousness, marked by Peribáñez's eventual rejection of those gifts, but simply in the transposition of his former relationship of subservience: Peribáñez and his wife, though freed from the personal domination of the Comendador, come willingly to accept for themselves the fact of their economic and social "humility." Casilda's initial profession of faith in the virtues of the peasant life,

> Más quiero yo a Peribáñez
> con su capa la pardilla
> que al Comendador de Ocaña
> con la suya guarnecida
>
> (771a)

(I love Peribáñez, with his humble brown cape, more than you, Comendador, with your embroidered one),

is internalized by Peribáñez as he is forced to repress his desire for the recognition bestowed upon him by the Comendador:

> Pienso que nos está bien
> que no estén en nuestra casa
> paños con armas ajenas:

> no murmuren en Ocaña
> que un villano labrador
> cerca su inocente cama
> de paños comendadores,
> llenos de blasones y armas.
> Timbre y plumas no están bien
> entre el arado y la pala,
> bieldo, trillo y azadón;
> que en nuestras paredes blancas
> no han de estar cruces de seda.
>
>   (776a–b)

(I think it is wrong for us to have such cloths hanging in our house, with someone else's arms on them. I would not have Ocaña whisper that a peasant surrounds his humble bed with noble hangings, covered with symbols of knighthood. Crests and plumes go ill with plows and shovels, forks and hoes. Our whitewashed walls should not be decorated with silk crosses.)

For Hegel, the dialectic of Master and Slave finds stabilization, if at all, in the family; the state, we know from the *Philosophy of Right,* is an extension of the family and its ethical bonds. In the *comedia,* however, familial relations are conspicuously absent, or are reduced to the same terms of absolute authority and obedience, self and other, good and evil, which we have seen to be characteristic of *Fuenteovejuna* qua romance. The literary and ideological closure which the *comedia* is able to achieve thus depends, as in the final scenes of *Fuenteovejuna* and *Peribáñez,* on the possibility of legitimizing the power of those who wield it—the father, the feudal lord, or the perfected image of these, the king. Yet this is precisely where the *comedia* most radically transforms the dialectic which Hegel proposed, by effacing the fact of social contradiction and thus resisting the process of historical change wrought by the need of newly constituted centers of power to legitimize themselves: especially where power becomes subject to the process of effacement, where the unavoidably political dimension is "demonized" in an effort to make it appear as though the subversion of the dominant order could come only from without—especially in such cases, the superiority of the master comes to depend on the willing submissiveness of the bondsman.[26]

Seen in such a light, the *comedia* becomes illuminating of a mode of "resistance to subjectivity" which is all the more remarkable insofar as it proceeds in a direction diametrically opposed to that which Deleuze and Guattari outlined in *L'Anti-Oedipe*. If Deleuze and Guattari advocate a strategy which would recover the energies of the divided consciousness and its heterogeneous desires in order to resist the tyranny of the oedipal triangle over modern existence, then the *comedia* offers resistance to the modernizing functions of capitalism by the most reactionary of means, viz., by the cultivation of what Foucault described as the "fascism within," the desire of the individual to seek his own domination (the town of Fuenteovejuna is described as leaderless—"sin capitán" [1845], yet it looks to submit itself to the authority of the King): it is from the satisfaction of this desire that the *comedia* derives the rhetorical force with which Lope credits it in the "Arte nuevo," its ability to please the masses, to "mover con fuerza a toda gente." By elaborating only slightly on Lope's terms, one might describe the *comedia* as a practice designed to provide pleasure in the repression of the very desires which it summons up: if the resistance to historical change implies the self-domination of the masses, then Lope's most important discovery was the fact that the psychology of the masses is to some extent always a fascist phenomenon, and that the resistance to historical change could best be achieved by making their domination a pleasurable experience.

Notes

[1]An earlier analysis of the seventeenth-century crisis is that of Roland Mousnier in the *Histoire générale des civilisations*. See also his contribution to "Trevor-Roper's 'General Crisis': A Symposium." Elliott's study of "decline" is anticipated by E. J. Hamilton ("The Decline of Spain").

[2]On absolutism in Spain, see Perry Anderson.

[3]See the essays and critical discussion of Maurice Dobb in Rodney Hilton. Lawrence Stone is useful for the case of England. In connection with Shakespeare in particular, see Rosalie Colie and Paul Delany.

[4]Hayden White qualifies this in relation to the Comic structure of Hegel's vision, which Marx sets out to rewrite:

Hegel's Comic conception of history was based ultimately on his belief in the right of life over death; "life" guaranteed to Hegel the possibility of an ever more adequate form of social life throughout the historical future. Marx carried this Comic conception even further; he envisioned nothing less than the dissolution of that "society" in which the contradiction between consciousness and being had to be entertained as a fatality for all men in all times. It would not, then, be unjust to characterize the final version of history which inspired Marx in his historical and social theorizing as a Romantic one. But his conception did not envisage humanity's redemption as a deliverance from time itself. Rather, his redemption took the form of a reconciliation of man with a nature denuded of its fantastic and terrifying powers, submitted to the rules of technics, and turned to the creation of a genuine community. (281–82)

The notion of romance as deliverance, and specifically as "deliverance from time," has been amply discussed in connection with Shakespearean drama by Northrop Frye.

[5]For two attempts to read the *comedia* as a means for the "direction" of the masses, see José Antonio Maravall, *Teatro y literatura,* and José María Díez Borque.

[6]González de Cellorigo, as cited in Elliott 184–85.

[7]González de Cellorigo, as cited in Vilar 66–67.

[8]Archivo General de Simancas, Hacienda leg. 395–547, Consulta of 3 September, 1617; cited in Elliott 186.

[9]The word "caste," which is Spanish in origin, did not carry the Hindu meaning, even though the Portuguese did later apply it to Indian society. See Américo Castro, *The Spaniards* 51.

[10]See Martin Green for this formulation.

[11]The late-fifteenth-century Spanish humanist Antonio de Nebrija defined caste as "good lineage." In the seventeenth century, Covarrubias explained that "caste means noble and pure lineage; he who comes from good family and descent, despite the fact that we say 'he is of good caste' or 'he is of bad caste.' . . . Those who are of good lineage and caste we call 'castizos.' " See Castro, *The Spaniards* 51.

[12]See Maravall's description of the "sociedad estamental" in connection with the *comedia* in *Teatro y literatura.*

[13]Castro is here radically revising his more conventional account of honor in the Golden Age published in "Algunas observaciones." See *De la edad conflictiva* 49ff.

[14]See Maravall's *Teatro y literatura* and also *La cultura del Barroco.*

[15]This notion is developed throughout Jameson's *The Political Unconscious.*

[16]On the generic repeatability of the *comedia,* see Díez Borque 357ff. ("Una estructura fija para unas funciones repetidas").

[17]Cf. Lawrence Manley.

[18]From the "Introduction" by Mark Seem xxi.

[19]The process is akin to that which Jonathan Dollimore has described as "containment," adopting Williams's rather than Jameson's sense: "Three aspects of historical and cultural process figure prominently in materialist criticism: consolidation, subversion, and containment. The first refers, typically, to the ideological means whereby a dominant order seeks to perpetuate itself; the second to the subversion of that order, the third to the containment of ostensibly subversive pressures" (10).

[20]Spitzer, "A Central Theme," 192. See also *Classical and Christian Ideas.*

[21]Casalduero's study was conceived as a reaction against Menéndez y Pelayo's nineteenth-century aesthetic, and marks the beginning of a Platonizing approach to the play from which Spanish criticism has been unable to clear free. Javier Herrero seeks to save the strictly political dimension of the play, but remains within the field of political theory rather than political praxis.

[22]See Jameson's discussion of Nietzsche's "deconstruction" of ethics, 114–17.

[23]That *Fuenteovejuna* is not written against the nobility as a class is evident from the fact that Lope provides for the regeneration of the young Master of the Order of Calatrava, Rodrigo Téllez Girón. There is some possibility that Lope may have favored the Master because of political connections between the Girones and the Osunas, Lope's patrons.

[24]Hobsbawm (*Primitive Rebels*) makes the following observation on the role of banditry, which helps shed light on its place in in early modern Spain:

The coming of the modern economy (whether or not it is combined with foreign conquest) may, and indeed probably will, disrupt the social balance of the kinship society, by turning some kins into "rich" families and others into "poor," or by disrupting the kin itself. The traditional system of blood-vengeance and outlawry may—and indeed probably will—"get out of hand" and produce a multiplicity of unusually murderous feuds and embittered outlaws, into which an element of class struggle begins to enter. (4)

Lope's *Pedro Carbonero* would repay further investigation in this light. See Avalle-Arce on this subject.

[25]For an illuminating discussion of this point, see Rosen 67–68.

[26]On effacement and legitimization in connection with Renaissance drama, see Dollimore:

Legitimization further works to efface the fact of social contradiction, dissent and struggle. Where these things present themselves unavoidably they are often demonised as attempts to subvert the social order. Therefore, if the very conflicts which the existing order generates from within itself are construed as attempts to subvert it from without (by the "alien"), that order strengthens itself by simultaneously repressing dissenting elements and eliciting consent for this action: the protection of society from subversion. (7)

Works Cited

ANDERSON, PERRY. *Lineages of the Absolutist State.* London: Versɔ, 1979.

ASTON, TREVOR, ed. *The Crisis in Europe 1560–1660.* New York: Basic, 1965.

AVALLE-ARCE, JUAN BAUTISTA. "Pedro Carbonero y Lope de Vega: Tradición y comedia." *Dintorno de una epoca dorada.* Madrid: José Porrúa Turanzas, 1979. 353–69.

CASALDUERO, JOAQUÍN. "*Fuenteovejuna.*" *Revista de filología hispánica* 5 (1943): 21–44.

CASTRO, AMÉRICO. "Algunas observaciones acerca del concepto del honor en los siglos XVI y XVII." *Revista de filología española* 3 (1916): 1–50, 357–86.

_____. *De la edad conflictiva.* Madrid: Taurus, 1972.

_____. *The Spaniards.* Trans. Willard King and Selma Margaretten. Berkeley and Los Angeles: U of California P, 1971.

COLIE, ROSALIE. "Reason and Need: *King Lear* and the 'Crisis' of the Aristocracy." *Some Facets of King Lear.* Ed. R. Colie and F. T. Flahiff. Toronto and Buffalo: U of Toronto P, 1974. 185–219.

DELANY, PAUL. "*King Lear* and the Decline of Feudalism." *PMLA* 91 (1977): 429–40.

DELEUZE, GILLES, and FELIX GUATTARI. *Anti-Oedipus: Capitalism and Schizophrenia.* Trans. Robert Hurley, Mark Seem, and Helen R. Lane. Minneapolis: U of Minnesota P, 1983.

DÍEZ BORQUE, JOSÉ MARÍA. *Sociología de la comedia del siglo XVII.* Madrid: Cátedra, 1976.

DOBB, MAURICE. *Studies in the Development of Capitalism.* London: George Routledge, 1946.

DOLLIMORE, JONATHAN. "Shakespeare, Cultural Materialism and the New Historicism." *Political Shakespeare: New Essays in Cultural Materialism.* Ed. Jonathan Dollimore and Alan Sinfield. Ithaca: Cornell UP, 1985. 2–17.

ELLIOTT, J. H. "The Decline of Spain." In *The Crisis in Europe,* ed. Trevor Aston. 167–73.

FRYE, NORTHROP. *The Myth of Deliverance.* Toronto: U of Toronto P, 1983.

GONZÁLEZ DE CELLORIGO, MARTÍN. *Memorial de la política necesaria y útil restauración de la república en España.* Valladolid, 1600.

GREEN, MARTIN. *Dreams of Adventure, Deeds of Empire.* New York: Basic, 1979.

HAMILTON, EARL J. "The Decline of Spain." *Economic History Review* 8 (1938): 168–79.

HEGEL, GEORG WILHELM FRIEDRICH. *The Phenomenology of Spirit.* Trans. A. V. Miller. New York: Oxford UP, 1977.

HERRERO, JAVIER. "The New Monarchy: A Structural Reinterpretation of *Fuenteovejuna.*" *Revista hispánica moderna* 36 (1970–71): 173–85.

HILTON, RODNEY, et al. *The Transition from Feudalism to Capitalism.* London: NLB, 1976.

HOBSBAWM, E. J. "The Crisis of the Seventeenth Century." In *The Crisis in Europe,* ed. Trevor Aston. 5–58.

———. *Primitive Rebels: Studies of Archaic Forms of Social Movement in the 19th and 20th Centuries.* New York: Norton, 1965.

JAMESON, FREDRIC. *The Political Unconscious.* Ithaca: Cornell UP, 1982.

LARSON, DONALD R. *The Honor Plays of Lope de Vega.* Cambridge: Harvard UP, 1977.

MANLEY, LAWRENCE. *Convention, 1500–1750.* Cambridge: Harvard UP, 1980.

MARAVALL, JOSÉ ANTONIO. *La cultura del Barroco.* Barcelona: Ariel, 1975.

———. *Teatro y literatura en la sociedad barroca.* Madrid: Seminarios y ediciones, 1972.

MCCRARY, WILLIAM C. "*Fuenteovejuna:* Its Platonic Vision and Execution." *Studies in Philology* 58 (1961): 179–92.

MOUSNIER, ROLAND, et al. *Histoire générale des civilisations.* Vol. 4. Paris: PUF, 1961.

———. "Trevor-Roper's 'General Crisis': A Symposium." In *The Crisis in Europe,* ed. Trevor Aston. 97–104.

ORTEGA Y GASSET, JOSÉ. *The Revolt of the Masses.* New York: Norton, 1960.

REICHENBERGER, ARNOLD. "The Uniqueness of the *Comedia.*" *Hispanic Review* 27 (1959): 303–16.

ROSEN, STANLEY. *G. W.F. Hegel: An Introduction to the Science of Wisdom.* New Haven: Yale UP, 1974.

SALOMON, NOËL. *Recherches sur le thème paysan dans la "comedia" au temps de Lope de Vega.* Bordeaux: Féret & Fils, 1965.

SEEM, MARK. Introduction. Deleuze and Guattari. xv–xxiv.

SPITZER, LEO. "A Central Theme and its Structural Equivalent in Lope's *Fuenteovejuna.*" *Hispanic Review* 23 (1955): 274–92.

_____. *Classical and Christian Ideas of World Harmony.* Baltimore: Johns Hopkins UP, 1963.

STONE, LAWRENCE. *The Crisis of the Aristocracy 1558–1641.* Oxford: Clarendon, 1965.

TÉLLEZ, FRAY GABRIEL [Tirso de Molina]. *El Burlador de Sevilla y convidado de piedra.* Ed. Joaquín Casalduero. Madrid: Cátedra, 1977.

TREVOR-ROPER, H. R. "The General Crisis of the Seventeenth Century." In *The Crisis in Europe,* ed. Trevor Aston. 59–95.

VEGA CARPIO, LOPE FELIX DE. "Arte nuevo de hacer comedias en este tiempo." Ed. Juan Manuel Rozas. *Significado y doctrina del "Arte nuevo" de Lope de Vega.* Madrid: Sociedad general española de librería, 1976. 181–94.

_____. *Fuenteovejuna.* Ed. Francisco López Estrada. Madrid: Castalia, 1969.

_____. *Peribáñez y el Comendador de Ocaña.* Ed. Federico Carlos Sainz de Robles. *Obras escogidas de Lope de Vega.* Vol. 1, Teatro. Madrid: Aguilar, 1969.

VILAR, PIERRE. "The Age of Don Quixote." *New Left Review* 68 (July–August 1971): 59–71.

VOSSLER, KARL. *Lope de Vega y su tiempo.* Trans. R. de la Serna. Madrid: Revista de Occidente, 1933.

WARDROPPER, BRUCE. "*Fuente Ovejuna: el gusto* and *lo justo.*" *Studies in Philology* 53 (1956): 159–71.

WHITE, HAYDEN. *Metahistory: The Historical Imagination in Nineteenth-Century Europe.* Baltimore: Johns Hopkins UP, 1973.

WILLIAMS, RAYMOND. *Marxism and Literature.* Oxford: Oxford UP, 1977.

WILSON, EDWARD. "Images et structures dans *Peribáñez.*" *Bulletin Hispanique* 51 (1949): 125–59.

The Beginnings of Elizabethan Drama: Revolution and Continuity

G. K. HUNTER

A STANDARD ASSUMPTION of literary history is that a group of young men, born of "middle-class" parentage in the 1550s and 1560s and graduating from Oxford or Cambridge between 1575 (Lyly) and 1588 (Nashe)[1] created between them the normal forms of Elizabethan Drama, casting behind them the primitive techniques and attitudes of preceding generations, designated "Tudor Drama," "Late Medieval Drama," or whatever other diminishing title distaste elects to supply. I call this assumption "standard" not because I seek to denigrate it (in the recurrent modern mode); there is much evidence that these young men perceived themselves, and were perceived by contemporaries, as constituting what would nowadays be called a radical movement and that the movement marked the beginning of something genuinely new. But the very obviousness of the general point leaves a number of supplementary questions unanswered because not asked. In particular I wish to ask the question *how* this group came to achieve their effect on drama.[2] The question is a purely instrumental one that does not seek to go beyond the evidence generally available in the words they wrote. This leaves, of course, the further issue of the status we give to these words. If we are to understand what the "University Wits" say as a simple description of the facts of the case, then we must suppose that it was expertise in classical culture that led to the creation of the new drama. But this connection seems to be part of the rhetoric of their social situation rather than expressive of any vital link that joins university culture to popular drama. I shall argue that the link can be seen more clearly in terms of the central issue of Elizabethan intellectual life—the theological debate about the relation of individual con-

29

science to the established hierarchies of the world. I shall argue that it was the perception of the individual voice as justified (in all senses of that word), even when socially isolated, that released the more obvious formal and literary powers we easily recognize. That the University Wits despised the popular theater they found when they came to London can hardly be disputed. The university milieu which had given them their claim to importance had anchored their sense of identity in the Humanist learning they had acquired there, their fluent command of a battery of Greco-Roman names, historical and fictional stories, self-conscious logical and rhetorical devices, tags and quotations, which provided the lingua franca of Humanist-educated Europe. In social terms these were, of course, means of defining an elite status, and they seem at first to offer only resistance to a demeaning function in popular entertainment, where (as Shakespeare was to point out) "nature is subdued / To what it works in, like the dyer's hand." Robert Greene more than once tells us how he suffered a sad decline into playwriting; and even though his narrative is more interesting as myth than as history it is worth pausing on. In *Francesco's Fortunes* (1590) we hear that Francesco (the Greene alternate) "fell in amongst a company of players, who persuaded him to try his wit in writing of comedies, tragedies, or pastorals, and if he could perform anything worthy of the stage, then they would largely reward him for his pains." And so Francesco "writ a comedy which so generally pleased all the audience that happy were those actors in short time that could get any of his works, he grew so exquisite in that faculty." (Greene 8: 128) In Greene's *Groatsworth of Wit* (1592) the story has become even more slanted. Roberto (the same hero, with another name) has come to an impasse in the Bohemian life he had thought to lead. He has been outsmarted and made penniless by the prostitute he planned to control. He is thrust out of doors, and sitting against a hedge he vents his wrath in English and Latin verses. On the other side of the hedge there happens to be a player, who now approaches Roberto:

Gentleman, quoth he (for so you seem), I have by chance heard you discourse some part of your grief . . . if you vouchsafe such simple comfort as my ability will yield, assure yourself that I will endeavour to do the best that either may procure your profit or bring you pleasure; the rather for that I suppose you are a scholar, and pity it is men of learning should live in lack.

Roberto, wondering to hear such good words . . . uttered his present grief, beseeching his advice how he might be employed. Why easily, quoth he, and greatly to your benefit; for men of my profession get by scholars their whole living. What is your profession, said Roberto. Truly sir, said he, I am a player. A player, quoth Roberto, I took you rather for a gentleman of great living, for if by outward habit men should be censured, I tell you you would be taken for a substantial man. So am I where I dwell (quoth the player) reputed able at my proper cost to build a windmill.

(12: 130–31)

The player goes on to indicate that he has greatly prospered by penning and playing folktales and moralities. "But now my almanac is out of date." He now needs a graduate, like Roberto, to catch the more sophisticated tastes of the present "in making plays . . . for which you shall be well payed if you will take the pains."

Roberto, perceiving no remedy, thought best to respect of his present necessity to try his wit and went with him willingly; who lodged him at the town's end [in a brothel]. . . . Roberto, now famoused for an arch-playmaking poet, his purse like the sea sometime swelled, anon like the same sea fell to a low ebb; yet seldom he wanted, his labors were so well esteemed.

(12: 132, 134)

His new profession earns him the much-needed money, but money earned under these circumstances is seen to be incapable of securing moral stability. Roberto so despises those from whom he earns his money that he can only define his difference from them by cheating them: "It becomes me, saith he, to be contrary to the world, for commonly when vulgar men receive earnest they do perform; when I am paid anything aforehand I break my promise" (Greene 12: 134). His money is spent among criminals and debauchees to support a way of life which produces execution for some and repentance before death for Roberto. It is at this point that Greene can proceed to warn "those gentlemen his quondam acquaintance that spend their wits in making plays" (Marlowe, Peele, [?Lodge/Nashe] and "two more that both have writ against these buckram gentlemen") to "never more acquaint them [the players] with your admired inventions" (Greene 12: 141, 144).

The story as thus told is a powerful one. But as far as the history of Elizabethan drama is concerned, the details leave much to be desired.

There is no evidence that Greene's dramatic talents had the electrify-
ing effect he describes. And we should note that he tells much the same
story about his prose romances of love. In *The Repentance of Robert
Greene* (1592) we hear not only that the "penning of plays" turned
him into a swearer and a blasphemer, but that

> These vanities [plays] and other trifling pamphlets I penned of love and vain
> fantasies were my chiefest stay of living, and for those my vain discourses I
> was beloved of the vainer sort of people who, being my continual compan-
> ions, came still to my lodgings, and there would continue quaffing, carousing
> and surfeiting with me all the day long.
>
> (12: 178)

Greene is much clearer about the status he is losing than about the
skills he is acquiring. He implies that all he has to do to succeed is to
turn his university-trained cleverness toward the writing of popular
literature and lo! he will grow "exquisite in that faculty." The extant
popular plays of Greene, Peele, and Lodge, however, do not at all support this idea; they are quite unlike any model the university could
have provided from the works of Seneca, Plautus, or Terence. In their
multitudes of characters, their wide range across space and time, their
carelessness of plot consistency, their interest in romantic love, their
reluctance to stay inside the boundaries of genre, their tendency to
heavy moralizing, such plays fit almost exactly the terms of neoclassical scorn with which Sir Philip Sidney had greeted the English plays of
the early 1580s. *James IV, Edward I, The Battle of Alcazar, Alphonsus
of Aragon,* and *A Looking Glass for London and England* all fall easily
under Sir Philip's rubric of "mongrel tragicomedy [with] some ex-
treme show of doltishness" (Sidney 135–36) and are in fact much
more like those warhorses of the popular stage, *Clyomon and Cla-
mydes* or *The Famous Victories of Henry V,* than they are like anything
in classical drama.

What, then, did the university contribute toward a new theatrical
creation that was not provided by a professional knowledge of the
stage? The evidence that contemporary comment provides is extraordinarily evasive. In the second part of the Cambridge play *The Return
from Parnassus* (1601–03) the graduates Philomusus and Studioso
seek to follow along the Greene path and try to secure employment as

actors and scriptwriters from the leading actors of Shakespeare's company, Burbage and Kemp. The brush-off they receive indicates some of the impediments that still lay, even in the next decade, in the path of those who sought to travel from a Humanist education to a career in the popular theater. Kemp tells the graduates: "Few of the university men plays well; they smell too much of that writer Ovid and that writer Metamorphosis and talk too much of Proserpina and Jupiter." (4.3.1766–68)

Kemp's entirely plausible expression of what we can recognize as the recurrent tension between the stage and the academy seems to be confirmed on the other side of the same coin by the rhetoric of self-definition that the Wits themselves indulge in. Nashe, for example, relies entirely on attainments in the classical languages to make his distinction between authentic and merely imitative playwrights. In his preface to Greene's *Menaphon* (1589) entitled "To the gentlemen students of both universities" Nashe tries to draw an impassible line between authentically learned men and those hangers-on or pretenders that he refers to ironically as "deep read schoolmen or grammarians," students, that is, who have never passed from the grammar school to the university. These will, he assumes, display the superficialities of a classical education; but it will be easy to detect them as outsiders masquerading as insiders, for they are "at the mercy of their mother tongue, that feed on naught but the crumbs that fall from the translator's trencher." These are essentially lower-class persons whose incapacities betray them as existing only at the intellectual level of the "serving man" or of the dealer in "commodities" (that is, the merchant). (Nashe 3: 312)

Nashe's attack on lower-class pretenders to learning becomes more specific in the famous following passage in which he deals with the kinds of plays that such grammar-school authors are capable of writing. Again, the central issue is ignorance of Latin: such men can "scarcely Latinize their neck-verse if they should have need"; they are the "famished followers" of "English Seneca" (often thought to refer to Thomas Newton's 1581 collection of Seneca's plays), because they are incapable of reading the original; and yet they "busy themselves with the endeavors of art" (Nashe 3: 313)—where "art" has the sense of specialized knowledge that is found in such phrases as "Master of Arts." It looks, from much of the reference in this passage, as if Thomas Kyd is the playwright most particularly aimed at. And indeed if *The Spanish Tragedy* came out in 1588 (as is often supposed) then Kyd must have provided in 1588/89 an obvious example of a nonuniversity playwright with a great theatrical success on his hands. The obvious objection to such identification is that *The Spanish Tragedy* has few if any of the characteristics specified; indeed it is unusually full of Latin verse, some of it, apparently, of Kyd's own composition, and if the play within the play was actually performed in "sundry languages" then it also contained considerable dialogue in French, Italian, and Greek as well. Such evidence, however, tells us little about the intention that prompted Nashe's words. "Grub Street hacks," "outsiders" are clearly necessary to the self-definition of any group seeking to lay claim to the "inside" position, and Nashe is no more likely to have been in search of accuracy and justice, when he attached names to labels, than Pope was in *The Dunciad.* If a Kyd had not existed, Nashe would have had to invent him (as, in the passage in question he very nearly did).

If Thomas Kyd was in fact merely a famished follower of authentic graduate playwrights, then it is a great gap in nature that we do not know who these men were or what they wrote; there are not even plausible candidates. It seems more rational to suppose that there were no such model playwrights; and this probability is reinforced by the parallel case of Shakespeare. Greene's famous 1592 attack on Shakespeare (12: 144) as yet another despicable outsider, jumped-up actor, and jack-of-all-trades ("Johannes fac totum"), pranking himself in the "feathers" he has stolen from the graduates, has no more detail of evidence to support it than appears in the case of *The Spanish Tragedy. Titus Andronicus* and *Richard III* are indeed plays that draw on a considerable, even if only grammar-school, acquaintance with the classics. If this derived from new work in drama by the University Wits, then once again one must note that the lines of filiation have disappeared. But it is more probable that the whole issue of "authentic" and "imitative" dramaturgy is only the fantasy of a socially insecure group of graduates, anxious to destabilize the opposition.

To deny the accuracy of such polemical rhetoric is not, however, to deny altogether the creative importance of this generation of University Wits in the history of Elizabethan drama, though it is certainly to deny their claim to tell the whole story in their own terms. One fact remains, which must not be underplayed or denied: the success of Marlowe's First Part of *Tamburlaine* (usually dated 1587) completely fulfilled the self-confidence of the group of graduates to which he belonged. Here at last we have a work of popular entertainment which openly claims classic status, whose presence visibly altered the landscape in which it appeared and charged its environment with new meanings. Of course, given the general lack of information, it is impossible to say that there were no popular plays like *Tamburlaine* written before *Tamburlaine;*[3] but the self-consciousness of innovation which pervades its language, the comments of contemporaries, the immediate appearance of imitations, all combine to tell us that this was seen as an originating event, even if it was so only because it was so seen. The originality of *Tamburlaine* was not noted primarily, however, in terms of dramaturgy. His contemporaries spoke of Marlowe as above all a poet, and the Prologue to *Tamburlaine* shows that Marlowe agreed with them. But the point being made is not only about versification, narrowly conceived; it is rather a point about the spirit that speaks through a poetry which is (as Michael Drayton was later to remark) "all air and fire" (3: 229) or (to quote Marlowe himself) "Like his desire, lift upward and divine." And this is, it will be noticed, a return to dramaturgy by the back door. For the theatrical function of a poetry as distinctive and powerful as that of *Tamburlaine* is to require of the auditor that he follow the action inside a particular given focus. In crude terms one can say that in *Tamburlaine* Marlowe presented the history of the outsider, the man of talents rather than of background, not in the traditional terms of social marginality but locked into a system of values where energy and desire are everything and need the great outside only to secure the greatest resonance "like the fa-burden of Bow bell," as Greene remarked (7: 8). Set against the hero's unfettered expression of individual will, the "insiders" of *Tamburlaine* are seen as passive, conformist, hesitant, as if only waiting to be taken over or destroyed by the individual whose force comes from believing in himself more than in anything outside.

It is time to ask the question how far the Marlovian vision and the Marlovian verse that conveys it are the product of a particular kind of education or representative of what we understand to have been the aspirations of the group of University Wits. Certainly there is little, if anything, in it that can be charged against imitation of classical authors read at university. But it is a mistake (as I have suggested above) to think that the focus of university education in this period was literary. The excitement of intellectual life in the sixteenth century came less from classical poetry than from the controversies of theology and from the techniques by which these could be conducted (see Kearney). From today's point of view the whole interest of such activities looks merely technical; but if we are to understand the excitement roused in the spirit of the times we can hardly afford to stop there. Clearly in such matters as the acceptance or rejection of sacraments, the belief or disbelief in the efficacy of works, the view taken on the mediation of the saints, the status of Purgatory, the function of vestments, we are dealing with the interlocking parts of total systems, where one false move can betray a whole understanding of the life of man, not only in eternity but in the daily life of earth as well. If the excitement of *Tamburlaine* can be seen to grow out of the intellectual energies generated in such disputes, then it becomes possible to argue that the play reflects its graduate generation at a deeper level than those we have so far considered.

Writing in 1588, Robert Greene spoke of the self-confident energy of Marlowe's verse as the expression of atheism: "daring God out of his heaven with that atheist Tamburlaine" (7: 8). Perhaps it is improper to make too much of the vocabulary used here. The context of the comment (Greene's jealousy of Marlowe's success) is not one likely to guarantee accuracy in the critical remark made. And "atheist" was in this period only a term of general abuse, with little necessary connection to specific doctrine (Febvre, ch. 2, sec. 6). On the other hand Marlowe was soon to acquire, and perhaps already had acquired, a considerable reputation as a freethinker. The idea that the power of *Tamburlaine* is directly connected to "atheism" may indeed point us toward more complex issues than are usually attached to Greene's scandals, for there are a number of interesting connections, which are largely obscured by the archaic vocabulary.

The more modern image of Marlowe is often presented in terms of that largely fictional genus "the Renaissance man"—Burckhardt's creatively amoral egotist, whether seen as artist (Aretino, Michelangelo,

Cellini) or as prince (Cesare Borgia, Julius II, Bernabo Visconti). But "Renaissance individualism," at least as it reached England, had rather different sources. And these take us back to the question of atheism once again. The key figures in such general growth of individualism as one can observe in England are neither artists nor the sacred monsters of royalty (egotism in the powerful is a characteristic so constant that it is hard to imagine it as having a history); they are rather the purveyors of reformed theology, Luther and Zwingli and Calvin and their native disseminators. The "Renaissance man" type of egotist who defines his individuality *against* orthodoxy is necessarily limited in the range of imitation he can inspire, for it is integral to his stance that he remain exceptional. Luther, however, and the other reformers, embodied individualism not against but inside orthodoxy, and indeed declared the sense of self to be the necessary basis of "true" orthodoxy. In this form the sense of the unique centrality of individual consciousness could penetrate throughout the culture of Europe to a degree not possible for the tyrants and exploiters of an older mode. And this was, as I say, the form in which "the Renaissance" pervaded England, so that, in England at any rate, the New Learning or Humanism inevitably explored classical forms and attitudes inside a world filled with the noise of challenge to intellectual conformity. In his search for justification by faith alone the individual could no longer hope to discover his identity by finding his place in any external system, for faith can only be felt and known inwardly. The doctrine of the slavery of the will (the *servum arbitrium*) required, paradoxically, that the individual remain in continued personal contact with the sources of God's Grace if he was to hope for eventual escape from the chains of Satan's power (Luther 327–32). The Reformed individual was thus continually caught up as protagonist in the largest and most terrifying drama that can be imagined, required to struggle and ask and decide and achieve, in a Satanic world, and without any external mediation. It would be surprising if this raw demand for extraordinary human capacity, marking the eventual irrelevance of external restraint, could be kept out of other areas of life, most significantly those where individual destiny must mean something more like secular fulfillment than loss of self in the Grace of God.[4] Of course, even the states which endorsed the Reformation struggled continuously against its antinomian tendencies, especially as these manifested themselves in political contexts. In England the hundred years or so between the 1530s and the 1640s saw a continuous effort to maintain system, order, consensus, in loyalty to the nation, the sovereign, the church, the tradition (as reinterpreted). Not all the weapons available to the state were equally effective, however. Nationalist fervor, suspicion of and contempt for foreigners, was a powerful means of securing consensus against the Pope, the Spaniards, and the Jesuits, but these positions were most powerfully argued by radical believers in the unmediated presence of Christ in the individual life. The corrosive solution that dissolved the foreign threat also ate into the English hierarchy.

The political argument against individualism was weakened on yet another front. The language of intellectual argument for loyalty inherited, inevitably, the language of Erasmian Humanism, of persuasion to civil order by the civilized consent of an educated elite (such as is addressed in the ironic mode of More's *Utopia,* for example) of finely disputable interpretations of uncertain texts (as in Erasmus's New Testament), of specialized and technical knowledge allowed to develop its own pragmatic justification ("arts" of war, health, navigation, algebra were all published in English in the fifties and sixties).[5] The English "Renaissance" book with probably the widest influence, Foxe's *Acts and Monuments* ("Foxe's Book of Martyrs") of 1563, was not only an epic of nationalism but also an epic of humble individualism (of widows, cooks, fishermen, brewers, and bricklayers, as well as scholars and clergymen) divinely justified in their rejection of the institutions of social control. The conflict depicted is not in the high romantic mode of *The Golden Legend,* set in exotic regions and the remote past. Foxe presents his readers with the recent and the local, describing lives rooted in the commonplaces of the ordinary and inculcating truth more by the evidence of shared experience than by any doctrinal argument. In all these cases, I would argue, a sense of the potential power of the unmediated individual, though disseminated primarily in religious terms, is bound to have created, in imagination at least, an idea that every self is capable of fulfillment and definition by resistance to conformity or convention. This is certainly the note in Elizabethan drama that we hear sounded clearly, for the first time, in *Tamburlaine.* The energetic individualism that appears in *Tamburlaine* has little or nothing to do with the "Renaissance individualism" of the late Quattrocento princes. Tamburlaine starts from nowhere and his dizzying rise to power is entirely self-generated out of assumptions that have nothing to support them in the world outside. He is totally free of the complacency of power, turning his eyes, as soon as he has achieved any one thing, to further horizons where he can test himself still further. The attitude of mind that is depicted here seems to be one that it is not inappropriate to consider as an atheistic version of the Lutheran soul in its search for justification through faith—atheistic because in this case the believer has simply excluded God from the equation and concentrated his faith on himself, at once justifier and justified.

If this was, in fact, the source of Marlowe/Tamburlaine's access of dazzling theatrical energy, his hunger for justification by power, it cannot surprise us that it was a source from which the other University Wits shrank back. They rushed to imitate the style, yet were voluble in their abhorrence of the beliefs of the man; and they seem not to have been too troubled by the contradiction. Presumably they took it that *Tamburlaine*'s lofty rejection of theatrical as of other conformism, and the new possibilities that this opened up for dramatic poetry, need bring only the *style* of self-assertion into fashion in the theater; they hoped to be able to spend Marlowe's legacy without remembering the means by which he had acquired it.[6]

By and large they were justified in their hope (as we shall see below). The history of Elizabethan drama is a history of compromises rather than of revolutions. But the initial revolution represented by *Tamburlaine* probably had to occur before the compromising could begin. Compromise is only likely to occur when two different systems of roughly equal weight and value are close enough to make exchange of elements a natural process. Greene's fulminations at the self-esteem of the acting fraternity do not open any path toward compromise: the values espoused by the two sides are too different to permit exchange. But when *Tamburlaine* had taken the stage by storm the Wits at last had a counter they could lay on the table. Of course we have no way of knowing how the negotiations proceeded, or if anyone was conscious that there was a process that might be called "negotiation." The evidence we possess suggests that no clones of *Tamburlaine I* could be produced; even *Tamburlaine II* represents a change of focus and a retreat into compromise. I have suggested that the other Wits took fright at the intellectual radicalism of Marlowe's play. One may also suspect that the innate conservatism of the theatrical institutions also exerted pressure toward a drama that might offer Tamburlainean excitement inside more traditional forms. What forms were these? Marlowe refers to his immediate predecessors as "rhyming mother wits"; but we cannot tell who these men were. There are, however, a few plays surviving from the decade before *Tamburlaine* that outline theatrical conditions that Marlowe seems to be flouting, quite deliberately, even while they deal with issues that Marlowe picks up (and changes).

The Conflict of Conscience, by Nathaniel Woodes, "Minister, in Norwich," is dated 1579 in the Malone Society Reprint, but 1572 (1570–81) in Harbage/Schoenbaum. In terms of technique the work could have been written at any time in the preceding fifty years; but its subject has a density and detail that mark the onset of the drama of particular lives. The hero, usually referred to as *Philologus,* represents, in fact, a real person, one Francis Spira, an Italian lawyer of the earlier part of the century who was persuaded to abandon the truths of Protestant doctrine and to revert to the falsehood of Catholicism; then, faced by the horror of the offense he had given to God and his conscience, he fell into despair and killed himself. Throughout the play we are shown the tragic destiny of the individual conscience, pressed on by the loss of everything that is desirable in the world—"fair children . . . wife most amiable . . . delicate diet . . . life lascivious," and by the certainty of the dungeon and the stake, "dolorous death which would me betray / And my felicity from me take away" (1596–1600). After interminable argument and temptation Spira proves unable to resist the pressure all around him. Then, of course, he has to face the opposite torment from within, and the certainty of not a temporary but an eternal loss. The rigorous logic of Spira's story (as told by Calvin and associates in 1549) is not, however, a logic that the dramatic form Woodes is using can sustain. He calls his play a "comedy" *(An excellent new comedy entitled The Conflict of Conscience, containing the most lamentable history of the desperation of Francis Spera, who forsook the truth of God's gospel for fear of the loss of life and worldly goods).* But for all the elasticity of the term "comedy" in the period

Woodes seems to have decided, at an early stage, to revise his work and evade the inexorable logic of the individual career.

In the first version of the play Woodes showed in Spira's suicide the logical consequence of his status as a mere "Philologus," that is someone "that loves to talk, / And common of the word of God, but hath no further care/ According as it teacheth them, in God's fear for to walk" (43–45), so that "Here may worldlings have a glass, their states for to behold" (2392). But at some point after the printing Woodes seems to have reconsidered the generic truth of what he had said in the Prologue: that

> a comedy will hardly him permit
> The vices of one private man, to touch particularly
> . . . .
> For if that SPERA had been one, we would straight deem in mind,
> That all by SPERA spoken were, our selves we would not find.
>
> (38–42)

The concern for immediate effect on an audience thus drives Woodes to insert cancel pages at the beginning and the end of his text, so that he can not only omit Spira's name but also provide comfort, even to "worldlings," by demonstrating that God can forgive sinners, though they may seem to be beyond Grace. In the new version Spira no longer commits suicide, but dies in God's time not his own. The pursuit of Christian consensus and the mode of "comedy" thus conspire together, as traditionally, to distort "the facts of the case." It looks as if the tragic potential of Spira's story could not at this time find any corresponding support in aesthetic or theatrical understanding; it is not until we come to Marlowe's handling of the parallel story in *Doctor Faustus* that we meet a capacity to handle individual rejection of consensus as tragic heroism.[7]

Woodes's play is an interesting historical document of the conflict between individual character on the one hand and the poetic range and dramatic form that the pre-*Tamburlaine* theater allowed, on the other hand. The plays of Robert Wilson demonstrate the nature of these theatrical constraints more effectively in terms of the achievements they made possible. Wilson was a well-known actor, one of the "twelve of the best" chosen in 1583 to be players for the queen, and noted in the account of this formation in Stowe's *Annals* (1615 edition) "for a quick, delicate, refined, extemporal wit" (Chambers 2: 349). As an actor-writer he was, presumably, one of that group that Greene and Nashe thought of as desperately anxious to buy the superior talents of the university graduates. Little sign of this appears, however, in the extant work. His *The Three Ladies of London* (1581)—probably his best play—shows his remarkable skill as a manipulator of theatrical responses, a skill that comes to life with particular vividness if we think of this play as not only a vehicle for his company (whatever it was at this time) but more particularly as providing a vehicle for himself in the role of the clown-raisonneur Simplicity. Simplicity, we should notice, is another outsider figure. But he is an outsider who has neither desire nor talent to become an insider. He is the rude but innocent countryman who reaches London without having any grasp on the nature of its capitalist activities and who is continually exploited by the devotees of Lady Lucre, whose corruptions he can perceive but whose dominance he is powerless to affect. Alone among the twenty-three speaking characters in the play Simplicity is never absorbed into the system ruled by Lucre; but this intransigence does not give him the status of a hero. Wilson indicates how easy it is to read Simplicity's innocence as ignorance, his naïveté as simplemindedness, his failure as his own fault. We may accept the doctrinal truth of what Simplicity says about the world, but we cannot identify with him (any more than we can identify with the Fool in *King Lear*). Like the Fool's, his career is a record of failure.[8] We leave him, toward the end of the action, being whipped for crimes he did not commit, while the well-placed criminals he has sought to expose look on and urge the need for exemplary punishment so that society can be properly protected. The eventual rescue of society from the vices of capitalism cannot come, we learn, from any of the characters inside the play. In the last scene a characterless "Judge Nemo" descends from heaven (as it were) and condemns everyone in sight. Simplicity's point of view is justified, but Simplicity is not around any more to enjoy the justification. The importance for the audience of the fact that this is a secular variant of the story of Christ's career in the world is obvious enough; but the political consequence should also be mentioned: the rescue of society, it is implied, cannot derive from any effort by any individual but will emerge from the operation of larger forces far outside human reach. The author and the audience can end the play in moral unison, but this is a unison in submission which flattens all the individual characters in the action.

Robert Wilson's *The Cobbler's Prophecy* of 1590 was probably performed at court (Chambers 3: 516), but it has few characteristics that mark it as exclusively courtly; and we may assume, I think, that it was performed also in the public theater. It offers an interesting companion-piece to *The Three Ladies of London,* especially if we allow the figure of Raph Cobbler to be another persona designed by Wilson for himself and therefore strictly comparable to Simplicity in the earlier play. The Cobbler is another bewildered prole, this time caught up by fiat of the Olympian gods into a prophetic eloquence which he pours out on rulers and wrongdoers alike. But, like Simplicity, Raph Cobbler remains very much a marginal figure as far as effective action is concerned. The effective movement to rescue society from the dalliance of Venus and Contempt (two versions of effeminacy) is supplied by Sateros, the soldier, who drives the whole action toward a morally rejuvenating war. The Cobbler, it seems, is going to end up punished (like Simplicity) for his violent and opinionated opposition to his social superiors, but he is pardoned at the last minute, and the gods restore him to proper humility as a working cobbler. Once again the author identifies himself with a truth-teller; but a truth-teller (even one with supernatural eloquence) is necessarily a marginal figure in terms of social restoration, constantly liable to get above himself, constantly endangered, and protected only by the jokes and ambiguities he shares with the audience (again like the Fool in *Lear*). The vices of society may be exposed in such ways, but social reform must come about by other means. The community that Simplicity or Raph Cobbler establish with the audience in the playhouse is a community of powerlessness, cemented by their joking together while they wait for the powers out of reach to make their unforecastable appearance. Simplicity and Raph Cobbler secure their powerful bond of comic consensus between the stage and the auditorium only because they present social vice from the essentially ineffective viewpoint of its victims. They show clowns to be better moralists than lords, but such subversions are essentially comic and collusive, easily accommodated inside the existing social hierarchy.

There is nothing here that corresponds to the University Wit voice of such a character as Nashe's Jack Wilton, equally powerless in his social role, but offering his readers, as it were, a way out of their standard subjection, the way of self-sufficient skepticism, even cynicism.[9]

The clearly understood relation between actor and audience in the popular theater of the eighties is shown with great clarity in the Prologue that Wilson wrote for *The Three Ladies of London*. Humble and undogmatic, Wilson leaves the decision about the kind of play he has written to the judgment of his auditors. Like the later (and markedly different) Prologue to *Tamburlaine,* Wilson begins by running through a number of the things that do not appear in his play. This is not a mythological nor yet a militaristic play, not one dealing with gods and devils, not a love play, not a pastoral or countrified play. What then? He defines it, in fact, only as a commercial play, one designed to please and so to sell. Its power to please is like that of a stall set up in front of a shop: there is a variety of goods that might attract customers, some one way, some another. But the decision, the "lead," he is careful to say, will always come from the customer, not the author.

The Prologue

To sit on honour's seat it is a lofty reach:
To seek for praise by making brags ofttimes doth get a breach.
We list not ride the rolling racks that dim the crystal skies,
We mean to set no glimmering glance before your courteous eyes:
We search not Pluto's pensive pit, nor taste of Limbo lake;
We do not show of warlike fight, as sword and shield to shake:
We speak not of the powers divine, ne yet of furious sprites;
We do not seek high hills to climb, nor talk of love's delights.
We do not here present to you the thresher with his flail,
Ne do we here present to you the milkmaid with her pail:
We show not you of country toil, as hedger with his bill;
We do not bring the husbandman to lop and top with skill:
We play not here the gardener's part, to plant, to set and sow:
You marvel, then, what stuff we have to furnish out our show.
Your patience yet we crave a while, till we have trimm'd our stall;
Then, young and old, come and behold our wares, and buy them all.
Then, if our wares shall seem to you well-woven, good and fine,
We hope we shall your custom have again another time.

To turn straight from Wilson's Prologue to *The Three Ladies of London* to Marlowe's Prologue to *Tamburlaine* is to move straight from the deference of the actor to the arrogance of the author, from pleading to command, from "clownage" to the "tragic glass," from "jigging veins of rhyming mother wits" to "high astounding terms." If theatrical excitement can be assimilated to the excitement of participating in a revolution (even if only a revolution of sensibility) then here indeed we find the revolution the Wits had been hoping for:

> From jigging veins of rhyming mother wits,
> And such conceits as clownage keeps in pay,
> We'll lead you to the stately tent of war,
> Where you shall hear the Scythian Tamburlaine
> Threat'ning the world with high astounding terms
> And scourging kingdoms with his conquering sword.
> View but his picture in this tragic glass,
> And then applaud his fortunes as you please.

Marlowe is not asking his audience to see if they can find anything attractive on his sedulously trimmed "stall." He will "lead" them, and they have no alternative but to follow. In some of the terms he uses Marlowe is clearly at one with Greene and Nashe: his "rhyming mother wits" are placed in the same category as Nashe's "deep read grammarians . . . at the mercy of their mother tongue"; but Marlowe, unlike his fellow graduates, moves directly from his condemnation of others to his demonstration of himself, exemplifying in the play that follows the overwhelming alternative he has to offer. Clownage, commercialism, vernacular limitation, lower-class verse forms, have all been swept away; in their place the audience will now be shown a "scene . . . more stately furnished than ever it was in the time of Roscius . . . not consisting . . . of a Pantaloon, a Whore and a Zany, but of Emperors, Kings, and Princes, whose true tragedies (*Sophocleo cothurno*) they do vaunt"—as Nashe in his *Pierce Peniless* (1592) described the new English stage (Nashe 1: 215). Marlowe's appeal to the audience (without which the play could not have been a success) is directed not toward identification with a familiar world endorsing familiar values but toward astonishment at finding oneself in free flight into the dangerous unknown. The audience is not to be reassured, but ev-

erywhere terrified, horrified, stimulated, by the discovery that this is
not a world in control but one in continual instability, one whose energies point not toward completion but only toward the further reaches
of desire.

The creative daring of *Tamburlaine*'s author, his clear intention to
defy theatrical orthodoxy, mirrors exactly the creative daring of his
hero. The destruction of social hierarchy inside the action finds external correspondence in the conquering rhetoric of the new mode of
theatrical projection. Author and hero may be "outsiders," but they
are not content to be understood as provincials or "clowns," having to
cling to the margins of "good society" for justification. The Reformation had given to every individual the possibility of a unique power as
the echo-chamber of the voice of God, and Humanism had added to
this the sense that the *novus homo* could become, by the transforming
power of education, the agent of cultural *renovatio*. Marlowe drew
on both these contemporary images by way of creative parody. Tamburlaine's declared confidence in himself as God's elected "scourge"
reinterprets conscience as a directive toward conquest, so that absolute power becomes the evidence of righteousness and divine favor.[10]

The writing of *Tamburlaine* thus answers, it would seem, the question I posed at the beginning of this essay. The sense of liberated individuality that Tamburlaine projects, and the accompanying invitation
to every individual in the audience to project his own fantasies of
Tamburlainean behavior—undoubtedly this created a new sense of
what the theater could do. The rash of conqueror plays that followed
show contemporary response to the liberation thus provided. Of
course there had been plays of tyrannic exorbitancy before this time.
But the older mode of *Cambyses* or *Apius and Virginia* dealt primarily with the decline of kingship when power becomes its own justification; the wickedness of such tyrants was represented as a collapse of
true humanity (under God) into an animal ferocity of desire. Following the lead of *Tamburlaine,* such plays as Greene's *Alphonsus, King
of Aragon,* Shakespeare's *Richard III,* Peele's *Alcazar,* the anonymous
plays *The True Tragedy of Richard III* and *Selimus,* deal with usurpation rather than tyrannic rule, with the rise rather than the fall of power. But in imitating *Tamburlaine* they change its mode. What they offer is the image of a world controlled by *Realpolitik,* through which

the outsider must make his way by appropriate treachery and manipulation, using a series of plots and deceptions to open up the cracks and mistrusts between members of the ruling clique. In *Tamburlaine* itself only the opening moves of the hero conform to this pattern: he allies himself with Cosroe to defeat Mycetes, and then, in possession of the army, he decides to overthrow Cosroe as well. But even in this move Tamburlaine is presented as more a force of natural selection than a plotter; and thereafter his opponents are arranged in a paratactic sequence, so that the emphasis lies on "the long majestic march and energy divine" rather than on the political process by which the victories are achieved. But the heroic energy of Marlowe's verse seems to be the one fuel able to sustain such movement; and after *Tamburlaine* even Marlowe himself seems disinclined to sustain that note. The other conqueror plays I have mentioned keep it only as a special effect. The weblike structure of power in any polity realistically considered requires the outsider who wishes to become an insider to move by a series of indirections, "with windlasses and with assays of bias," as Polonius describes it (*Hamlet* 2.1.65–66). In such structures grand gestures are ruled out, almost of necessity. The edifice of resident power can only be brought down by concealment, cunning, and apparent humility. And so something of the pre-*Tamburlaine* dramaturgy comes to be reinstated. The spectacle of great criminal careers that derive from Marlowe continues to invite an appalled identification from the audience, but the method of identification has slipped a couple of notches. In Marlowe's Guise or Barabas, in Richard III or Selimus, we find our attention engaged once again with the wiles of the Tudor Vice figure, whose abstracted characteristics have now been integrated into the psychological processes of *Realpolitik* (see Spivack). Another aspect of this is the return to "clownage," to the "fond and frivolous gestures" that *Tamburlaine* (as printed, at least) was supposed to have sent into exile.[11]

As I have said, no doubt some of the pressure leading to this turn from revolution to compromise came from the institution of the theater itself, from the despised actors that Greene had represented as existing at an intellectual dead-end, and in desperate need of the new drama that only the graduate generation could supply. The generation of the University Wits certainly did have an effect on the history of the

Elizabethan drama: plays with an analytic and political view of the historical process achieved popularity (*The Massacre at Paris, The Battle of Alcazar,* for example), though without altogether displacing chivalric romance—remember that *Mucedorus* was the most reprinted play of the era. The hybrid Moralities largely withered away. The clumsily moving and heavily moralistic fourteener (whose predictable rhythms seem to have been specially designed to carry clichés) was abandoned in favor of the expressionistic power of speech-accented blank verse. In all these aspects the generation of the middle nineties inherited a remade medium. But in other ways, many of them central and inescapable, the revolution was only fulfilled to the degree that the French Revolution was fulfilled by the reign of Louis Philippe. A structure of highly various, loosely connected scenes, here Asia, there Africa, drawing on a wide range of characters and events, some high-class, some low, some comic, some tragic, continued to provide the staple fare. Shakespeare offers us *Realpolitik* but flanks it with clown comedy; and at the end of his career he is willing to return to the jigging veins of Gower and the humble self-exculpations of Time. Behind the changes a deep continuity continues to manifest itself.

If we are surprised at this development it is mainly because we bring an inappropriate focus to bear. The history of Elizabethan drama is normally written as part of the history of literature or else as an aspect of intellectual history; but it is less either of these than it is the history of specific institutions, of the theatrical companies, their economic practices, their buildings, their relationships to the centers of power and patronage. The University Wits sought to change the conditions of playwriting, for good authorial reasons; they sought to redefine it as an activity that would allow them to impose their literary values on the extant institutions. In such matters, however, individuals may propose, but institutions dispose. And institutions seldom accept change unless there are good institutional reasons for doing so (decline in profits, problems of public order, trouble with censorship). At a later point in the story it may well be that the literary taste of the court may have had an effect on such popular playwriting as might reach the court. But at the dates we are considering this does not seem to be an important factor. In the generation of the University Wits, if the graduates were to make any headway in the popular theater, they had to learn to live inside the requirements of its trade. The trade, no doubt, was content to accept the up-market elements that graduate writers could supply, so long as they stayed inside the traditional popular forms that actors knew how to manage and that the public was used to. The ambition to move outside these constraints required for its fulfillment nothing less than a new cultural milieu.

Notes

[1]The dates we know (or believe on the basis of good evidence) are as follows:

Lyly	born 1554	graduated 1575 M.A.
Peele	born 1557	graduated 1579 M.A.
Lodge	born 1557	graduated 1577 B.A. +
Greene	born 1558	graduated 1583 M.A.
Marlowe	born 1564	graduated 1587 M.A.
Nashe	born 1567	graduated 1586 B.A. +

The phrase "graduated B.A. + " is used to indicate that the student took the B.A. in that year and stayed on at the university, but did not graduate M.A.

[2]See, for example, Salingar, who describes how "actor's companies, employing the University wits, established the technical conventions of Elizabethan staging, which remained broadly similar from the building of the first playhouse in 1576 to the closing of the theatres in 1643" (2, 66). The nomenclature used to describe the periods is, of course, very mixed. In *English Drama*, ed. Wells, the period before Marlowe is called· "Tudor and Early Elizabethan Drama" (no distinction between these two being observable inside the chapter). In vol. 5 of *The Cambridge History of English Literature* tragedy up to *Selimus* (1592) and *Locrine* (1591) is called "Early English Tragedy."

[3]The word "popular" must be stressed in this context. J. P. Brawner in his edition of the anonymous *The Wars of Cyrus* (1942) has argued that the Marlovian versification of this play should be dated some ten years before *Tamburlaine*. But *The Wars of Cyrus* is a courtly play designed for performance by singing boys. Academic tragedy in Latin (such as Richard Legge's *Richardus Tertius*, c. 1580, and the anonymous *Solymannidae* of 1582) offers precedents, but once again in a very different medium.

[4]The social liberation that Reformed doctrine could provide under certain circumstances has been discussed most commonly in terms of capitalist enterprise, as in Weber, and Tawney.

[5]Robert Recorde, *The Castle of Knowledge* (1556) and *The Whetstone of Wit* (1557)—the latter dealing with algebra; Thomas Tusser, *A Hundred Good Points of Husbandry* (1557); William Bullein, *The Government of Health* (1558); Peter Whitehorne [translating Machiavelli], *The Art of War* (1560); Richard Eden [translating Cortes], *The Art of*

Navigation (1561); William Bullein, *A Bulwark against All Sickness* (1562); Richard Rainolde [translating Aphthonius], *The Foundation of Rhetoric* (1563); William Bullein, *A Dialogue against the Fever Pestilence* (1564); Humphrey Baker, *The Wellspring of Sciences* (1568)—dealing with arithmetic.

[6]The style alone was sufficient to raise strong moral and social objections. The third satire of the first book of Joseph Hall's *Virgidemiarum* (1598) gives a full account. Hall charges that those whom Ben Jonson was later to describe as "the ignorant gapers" at *Tamburlaine* (Jonson, VIII, 587) will be morally damaged by identifying with the hero: "some upreared, high-aspiring swain . . . doth set his soaring thought / On crowned kings . . . As it might be the Turkish Tamburlaine. / Then weeneth he his base drink-drowned spright / Rapt to the three-fold loft of heaven's height, / When he conceives upon his feigned stage / The stalking steps of his great personage, / Graced with huff-cap terms and thundering threats / That his poor hearers' hair quite upright sets . . . Now swooping inside robes of royalty / That erst did scrub in lousy brokery."

[7]In "*Dr. Faustus:* A Case of Conscience," Lily B. Campbell conducts an extended comparison of these two plays.

[8]For an interesting and relevant comment on the social role of the Fool character see Weimann.

[9]I believe that there is no need to argue the inappropriateness of such a controlling cynicism in the theatrical context of that period.

[10]The role of Tamburlaine as the "scourge of God" has been most elaborately treated in Battenhouse, but in terms opposite to those proposed here.

[11]See the preface to *Tamburlaine* by the printer (Richard Jones)—"To the gentlemen readers and others that take delight in reading histories: I have purposely omitted and left out some fond and frivolous gestures, digressing and, in my poor opinion, far unmeet for the matter, which I thought might seem more tedious unto the wise than any way to be regarded, though haply they may have been of some vain-conceited fondlings greatly gaped at what time they were showed upon the stage in their graced deformities."

Works Cited

BATTENHOUSE, ROY W. *Marlowe's "Tamburlaine": A Study in Renaissance Moral Philosophy.* Nashville: Vanderbilt UP, 1941.

BRAWNER, J. P., ed. *The Wars of Cyrus.* Illinois Studies in Language and Literature 28: 3–4. Urbana: U of Illinois P, 1942.

CAMPBELL, LILY B. "Dr. Faustus: A Case of Conscience." *PMLA* 67 (1952): 219–39.

CHAMBERS, E. K. *The Elizabethan Stage.* 4 vols. Oxford: Clarendon, 1923.

DRAYTON, MICHAEL. "To my most dearly loved friend, Henry Reynolds, Esquire." *The Works of Michael Drayton*. Ed. J. W. Hebel and K. Tillotson. 5 vols. Oxford: Blackwell, 1934–41.

FEBVRE, LUCIEN. *La probleme de l'incroyance au xvi^e siecle*. Paris: Michel, 1942.

GREENE, ROBERT. *The Life and Complete Works in Prose and Verse*. Ed. Alexander B. Grosart. 15 vols. Printed for private circulation only, 1881–86.

HALL, JOSEPH. *Poems*. Ed. Arnold Davenport. Liverpool: Liverpool UP, 1949.

JONSON, BEN. *Works*. Ed. C. H. Herford and Percy and Evelyn Simpson. 11 vols. Oxford: Clarendon, 1925–52.

KEARNEY, HUGH F. *Scholars and Gentlemen: Universities and Society in Pre-Industrial Britain 1500–1700*. London: Faber, 1970.

LUTHER, MARTIN. *On the Bondage of the Will. Luther and Erasmus: Free Will and Salvation*. Ed. Philip S. Watson and B. Drewery. Philadelphia: Westminster, 1969.

MARLOWE, CHRISTOPHER. *The Plays*. Ed. Roma Gill. London: Oxford UP, 1971.

NASHE, THOMAS. *The Works*. Ed. R. B. McKerrow. 5 vols. London: Sidgwick and Jackson, 1904–10.

The Three Parnassus Plays. Ed. J. B. Leishmann. London: Nicholson and Watson, 1949.

SALINGAR, LEO. "The Elizabethan Literary Renaissance." *A Guide to English Literature*. Ed. Boris Ford. Harmondsworth: Penguin, 1955.

SIDNEY, PHILIP. *An Apology for Poetry*. Ed. Geoffrey Shepherd. London: Nelson, 1965.

SPIVACK, BERNARD. *Shakespeare and the Allegory of Evil*. New York: Columbia UP, 1958.

TAWNEY, R. H. *Religion and the Rise of Capitalism*. London: Murray, 1926.

WARD, A. W. and A. R. WALLER, eds. *The Cambridge History of English Literature*. 15 vols. Cambridge: Cambridge UP, 1907–27.

WEBER, MAX. *The Protestant Ethic*. New York: Scribner, 1930.

WEIMANN, ROBERT. *Shakespeare and the Popular Tradition in the Theater*. Baltimore: Johns Hopkins UP, 1978.

WELLS, STANLEY, ed. *English Drama: Excluding Shakespeare*. London: Oxford UP, 1975.

WILSON, ROBERT. *The Cobbler's Prophecy,* 1594. Ed. A. C. Wood. Oxford: Malone Society Reprints, 1914.

_____. *The Three Ladies of London,* 1590. Vol. 6 of Dodsley's *Select Collection of Old English Plays.* Ed. W. C. Hazlitt. 15 vols. London: Reeves and Turner, 1874–76.

WOODES, NATHANIEL. *The Conflict of Conscience,* 1581. Ed. Herbert Davis and F. P. Wilson. Oxford: Malone Society Reprints, 1952.

Subjectivity, Sexuality, and Transgression: The Jacobean Connection

JONATHAN DOLLIMORE

A NY STUDY of transgression finds itself, of necessity, and soon, asking some searching questions—e.g.: does transgression primarily
refer to an action, a social practice, or even more generally still, the
struggle to produce alternative cultures and knowledges? How do we
assess its success or failure? And who is "we"? Who decides whether
transgression is regressive or progressive, revolutionary, or reactionary—or neither? Such a study raises questions which invite—demand
perhaps—a materialist analysis, by which I mean an analysis which
seeks to be theoretically rigorous, historically aware, and politically
involved.

Issues of transgression are inextricably bound up with those of subjectivity, and if poststructuralism enables us better to understand
transgression in the Renaissance, this is perhaps because its conceptions of subjectivity are actually closer to those found in the Renaissance than is commonly reckoned. Often, essentialist conceptions of
the self which only take effective hold in the Enlightenment and are
then subsequently developed within Romanticism and Modernism,
have been erroneously aligned with those in the Renaissance. Consider for example that great imperative of the Renaissance, *Nosce teip-*

sum, know thyself. Today, for poststructuralism, know thy discursive formations. But surely in the Renaissance also: terminology apart, did not *nosce teipsum* mean something like that? Though it has generally been appropriated by humanist criticism as a recognizable origin of itself, it may nevertheless have something crucial in common with the formulations of poststructuralism. Of the few central beliefs uniting the various poststructuralisms (and connecting them with postmodernism) this is one of the most important: human identity is more constituted than constitutive; constituted by, for example, the preexisting structures of language and ideology, and by the material conditions of human existence. Thus is the subject decentered, and subjectivity revealed as a kind of subjection—not the antithesis of social process but its focus.

In the Renaissance also the individual was seen as constituted by and in relation to—even the effect of—a preexisting order. To know oneself was to know that order. There is most obviously perhaps the tripartite division of the soul, a model inherited from classical culture and undergoing various further subdivisions in the intervening centuries. And as regards being an effect of a prior order we need only consider Richard Hooker's declaration: "God hath his influence into the very essence of all things, without which influence . . . their utter annihilation could not choose but follow" (2:26). Or the commonplace with which Sir John Davies begins his *Nosce Teipsum*: God wrote the law directly into the hearts of our first parents. Hooker concurs: the law of Reason, the universal law of mankind, is "imprinted" in men's souls and "written in their hearts" (1:166,228). And when Montaigne and Bacon stress the determining power of social custom, they are developing the same idea of an order prior to and determining of the individual, though now of course with the crucial difference that it is a nonteleological order, historical rather than divine, material rather than metaphysical.[1]

Obviously there are far-reaching differences between Renaissance metaphysics and poststructuralism. For one thing the Renaissance view of identity as constituted (metaphysically) was also and quite explicitly a powerful metaphysic of social integration. In other words, to be metaphysically identified was simultaneously to be socially positioned—the subject in relation to the Prince, the woman in relation to the man, and so on. Metaphysics here underpins a discursive formation of the subject, of subjection. This link between subjectivity and subjection, which for poststructuralism has to be disclosed before it can be resisted, is, by comparison, both made explicit and endorsed in the Renaissance. Another difference: within Renaissance metaphysics a constituted identity might nevertheless be essentially fixed (e.g., the soul as divine creation) in a way that poststructuralism would also reject (identity is not only constructed but contingently so). Despite these differences, however, poststructuralism is helping us to see again what the Renaissance already knew: identity is in-formed by what it is not. It also helps us to see that if (as was apparent in the early seventeenth century) identity is clearly constituted by the structures of power, of position, allegiance, and service, any disturbance within or of identity could be as dangerous to that order as to the individual subject. Hooker, in a now famous passage, asked: "see we not plainly that obedience of creatures unto the law of nature is the stay of the whole world?" (1:157). Equally plain of course is that in this view disobedience is literally world shattering. The metaphysical construction of subjectivity is also an admission—and production—of its disruptive potential, a disruption in and of the very terms of its construction. A conception of the self as socially and/or metaphysically constituted produces one idea of transgression while a conception of the self as essentially (if not socially) unified and autonomous, quite another. That difference is addressed in what follows.

II

Lillian Faderman, in her book *Surpassing the Love of Men* (ch. 4), records two separate cases of women in France who in the sixteenth century were punished for using transvestite disguise and deploying dildos in their lesbian relations.[2] From one modern point of view these women's transgression is deeply suspect. I'm not referring to the conservative perspective which condemns sexual deviance per se, but to another perspective, one which might actually endorse deviance in principle, at least if it were seen as a quest for authentic selfhood. But here, precisely, is the problem; even (or especially) from this radical perspective, the women's behavior was inauthentic, not truly transgressive: in their use of men's clothing and the dildo they were

trying to imitate precisely that masculine order which they should
have been transcending. This, then, was regressive, not progressive,
false, not true consciousness. Compare the heroine of *Rubyfruit Jungle* (1973) who articulates the perspective in question when confronted with a butch/femme lesbian bar: "That's the craziest, dumbass thing
I ever heard tell of. What's the point of being a lesbian if a woman is
going to look and act like an imitation man? Hell, if I want a man, I'll
get the real thing not one of these chippies" (Brown 47–48). Or again,
the anonymous interviewee cited by Esther Newton: "I hate games! I
hate role playing! It's so ludicrous that certain lesbians, who despise
men, become the exact replicas of them!" (7).

But the question remains: why were those two French women in the
sixteenth century found so threatening? One of them was sentenced to
be burned and the other hanged, punishments dictated, apparently,
not by their lesbianism per se but their transvestism and use of the
dildo—*at once*, I want to suggest, appropriations of masculinity, in-
versions of it, and substitutions for it.

The kind of transgression whose test they retrospectively failed,
namely, transgression as a quest for authenticity, has been a powerful
idea from romanticism through modernism and into the sexual revolution. Underpinning and endorsing the philosophy of individualism,
it suggests that in defying a repressive social order we can dis-cover
(and so be *true* to) our *real* selves. Its view of human subjectivity is essentialist. Moreover it affirms that truth and reality are profoundly
subjective, inextricably bound up with the essential self. For conve-
nience and only provisionally I call this idea of transgression humanist. Clearly it is rooted in the essentialist humanism generated by the
Enlightenment and undergoing various mutations ever since. And in
our own century, it stems from what might fairly be called a radical humanism. Consider one of its classic expressions, André Gide's *The Immoralist* (1902). In that novel sexual transgression becomes a quest
for the essential self. Its hero, Michel, throws off the culture and learning which up to that point have been his whole life, in order to find
himself, "the authentic creature that had lain hidden beneath it . . .
whom the Gospel had repudiated, whom everything about me—
books, masters, parents, and I myself had begun by attempting to suppress. . . . Thenceforward I despised the secondary creature, the crea-

ture who was due to teaching, whom education had painted on the surface" (51). He composes a new series of lectures in which he shows "Culture, born of life, as the destroyer of life" (90). The true value of life is bound up with individual uniqueness: "the part in each of us that we feel is different from other people is just the part that is rare, the part that makes our special value" (100). Here, effectively, the self is understood in terms of a presocial, individuated essence, nature, and identity, and on that basis is invested with a quasi-spiritual autonomy. Culture has repressed this authentic self, and the individual embarks on a quest to recover it, a quest which is an escape from culture.

The significance for our culture of humanist transgression, this escape from repression into the affirmation of one's true self, can hardly be overestimated. Contrary to what has sometimes been implied, it didn't appear with existentialism; nor did it disappear when that movement ceased to be fashionable. And its prevalence has led us to misconceive both the significance and practice of transgression in earlier periods, especially the Renaissance, and even in some of our own contemporary subcultures. What intrigues me about that earlier period, especially its drama, is a mode of transgression which finds expression through the inversion[3] and perversion of just those preexisting categories and structures which humanist transgression seeks to transcend, to be liberated from; a mode of transgression which seeks not an escape from existing structures, but rather a subversive reinscription within them—and in the process a dis-location of them. I call this, again provisionally, transgressive reinscription. Examples preliminary to the main instances which follow might include the malcontent who haunts the very power structure which has alienated him, seeking reinscription within it but at the same time demystifying it, operating within and subverting it at the same time; the revengers whose actions constitute an even more violent bid for reinscription within the very society which has alienated and dispossessed them; the assertive woman, the woman on top,[4] who simultaneously appropriates, exploits, and undermines masculine discourse.

Humanist transgression in the name of authenticity has never been able to comprehend this other kind of transgression, that performed in the name of inversion, perversion, and reinscription. Moreover humanist transgression has proved wanting. Marked indelibly with the traces of idealist culture, it was perhaps inevitable that it should prove wanting. Inevitable, too, that in the wake of its failure we should become deeply skeptical about the very possibility of transgression. Because, in the words of Michel Foucault, "there is no single focus of great Refusal, no soul of revolt, source of all rebellions, or pure law of the revolutionary" (95–96)—because of that, there now seems to be only law itself, coercively or ideologically at work: coercively in the sense of being actively and increasingly repressive, ideologically in the sense of actively preempting resistance and subversion because somehow preceding and informing them. And so in recent years we have become preoccupied with the so-called containment of transgression—not merely its defeat by law, but its production and harnessing by law for law's own ends.

There is, for example, a functionalist argument to the effect that transgression may only be licensed, a kind of ritual safety valve which, far from undermining the existing order, actually reinforces it. Then there is the psychological version of this argument: paradoxically the sacred is most valued by the sacrilegious, and real faith lies in honest doubt. This argument includes Richard Sennett's notion of disobedient dependence, a defiance presupposing the very dependence it is trying to subvert, and in which "transgression is perhaps the most important element." This is a defiance based upon dependence, a rebellion not so much against authority as within it; the transgressor indeed disobeys but authority regulates the terms. As such this form of disobedience "has very little to do with genuine independence or autonomy . . . the world into which a person has entered through the desire to transgress is seldom however a real world of its own, a true alternative which blots out the past" (Sennett 33–34).[5] Sennett's argument might then be broadly supported by a structuralist or indeed poststructuralist argument to the effect that transgression, especially transgressive inversion, too often remains within—i.e., *merely* reverses—the binary opposition which structures both it and the law being contravened. (This would be the critique, in theoretical guise, of the "mannish" lesbian.) There are, then, at least three versions of this powerful argument whereby transgression is contained.

Stephen Greenblatt engages with such arguments in his seminal studies of authority and subversion. In *Renaissance Self-Fashioning*, a book which marks an immensely rewarding contribution to Renaissance studies, he argues that Marlowe's heroes remain embedded in what they oppose: "they simply reverse the paradigms and embrace what the society brands as evil. In so doing, they imagine themselves set in diametrical opposition to their society where in fact they have unwittingly accepted its crucial structural elements." In *Faustus* "the blasphemy pays homage to the power it insults" (209, 212). Greenblatt has in mind here that extraordinary moment when Faustus seals his pact with the devil by uttering Christ's dying words on the cross: "consummatum est." Faustus willfully ends himself; he sells his soul to the devil. Creation recoils; his blood congeals. Via the expression of a perverse masochism, with its disturbing mix of abjection and arrogance, this act, in one sense the supreme antithesis of everything Christ died for—he died after all to save us all—is identified with Christ. Is not this transgression contained, the unintended reverence paid by the sacrilegious to the sacred? Or is it rather a transgressive reinscription, a demonic perversion of the sacred? And what else (one might be led to wonder) was Christ in his death but the keenest image of abjection and arrogance, that transgressive masochism which has played such an important part in making and unmaking our culture, not least in the figure of the martyr, and which figures over and again in the cultural depictions of the crucifix? Faustus violates Christianity in the name and image of Christ; assimilating Christ to his opposite he thereby discloses the possibility that this opposite may be latent within Christ. Similarly, as I've argued elsewhere (Dollimore, *Radical Tragedy* ch. 6), this play associates God with his antithesis, with those secular tyrants who, in contemporary reality, were legitimating themselves in the name and image of God. What we witness here is something resembling the Freudian proposition that the repressed returns via the very images, structures, and mechanisms of repression itself: the words which consummate the renewal of man, his salvation, these words return to signify the opposite of salvation which is damnation, and they signify also the desire which only damnation can acknowledge and which salvation must repress. If it makes sense to think of evil as the repressed of Christianity, then this process also constitutes the return of the repressed in the supreme image of its repression: the dying Christ.[6]

I want to suggest that what is overlooked, both in humanist transgression and in some recent arguments for the inexorable containment of transgression, is the part played by contradiction and dis-location in the mutually reactive process of transgression and its control. I'm using the term contradiction in its materialist sense to denote the way social process develops according to an inner logic which simultaneously, or subsequently, effects its negation. Three paradigms of this derive from Hegel, Marx, and Freud—Hegel's theory of the master/slave dialectic, Marx's theory of the fundamental contradiction between the forces and relations of production, and the Freudian proposition just referred to, namely, the return of the repressed via the mode of its repression. In a revolutionary conjuncture contradictions may contribute to the disintegration of an existing order, though only (usually) through terrible suffering and struggle. That has to be said. In a nonrevolutionary conjuncture contradictions render social process the site of contest, struggle, and change. And, again, suffering. The contradictions which surface in times of crisis are especially revealing: they tell us that no matter how successful authority may be in its repressive strategies, there remains something potentially uncontrollable not only in authority's *objects* but in its *enterprise*, its rationale, and even its origin.

Deviancy, whether of Faustus's kind or that of the transvestite, plays a revealing part here, both as that which becomes especially visible in times of crisis, and that which focuses the inherent contingency of, and potential contradictions within, power. This is why we are mistaken if we think that deviancy exists outside of the dominant order. Though socially marginal the deviant remains discursively central: though an outcast of society s/he remains indispensable to it. For example: the process of identifying and demonizing deviance may be "necessary" to maintaining social order, either in the sense that deviancy poses an actual threat, or that it is perceived as threatening, or that a prevailing authority is able to relegitimate itself through that process of identifying and demonizing deviance. In practice these three responses to deviance are rarely separable.

Taking the example of deviancy, consider another but quite different instance of transgressive reinscription. The late Gāmini Salgādo once described the vagabonds of the Elizabethan low-life pamphlets as follows:

Seen through the disapproving eyes of respectable citizens they were nothing but a disorderly and disorganized rabble, dropouts from the social ladder. But seen from within, they appear to be like nothing so much as a mirror-image of the Elizabethan world picture: a little world, tightly organised into its own ranks and with its own rules, as rigid in its own way as the most elaborate protocol at court or ritual in church. (13)

From the respectable view, then, these rogues were merely the dregs of civilization—potentially dangerous, it's true, but in no way a part of the real social order. From another view they comprise a mirror-image of that order. But if the second view is accurate, do not the rogues become another clear instance of transgression contained, of a subculture which has internalized the structures and values of the dominant culture? Are they not paradoxically reproducing the laws which exclude and oppress them, even as they seem to be escaping and subverting those laws? Not exactly, because this very mimickry of the dominant involves a scandalous inversion. In the words of one contemporary observer: "these cheaters turned the cat in the pan, giving to diverse vile patching shifts an honest and godly title, calling it by the name of law . . . to the destruction of the good labouring people" (Salgādo 15). And feeding back through that inversion is an equally scandalous interrogation of the dominant order being mimicked; civil society is itself shown to be rooted in a like corruption. If this subculture imitates the dominant from below, it also employs a strategy whereby it undermines the dominant. Even as civil society endlessly displaces corruption from the social body as a whole onto its low-life (this in all likelihood corresponding to the first view above, that of the respectable citizens who see the low-life as society's waste product), the latter reveals both the original source and full extent of corruption within the dominant itself (Salgādo 16, 174). Inversion becomes a kind of transgressive mimesis: the subculture, even as it imitates, reproducing itself in terms of its exclusion, also demystifies, producing a knowledge of the dominant which excludes it, this being a knowledge which the dominant has to suppress in order to dominate.

In summary, then: change, contest, and struggle in part are made possible by contradiction and focused internally through deviancy. For all their differences both Foucault and Derrida lend support to this argument. Foucault, in the *History of Sexuality*, speaks of resistance not as outside power but inscribed within it as its irreducible opposite

(96). And Derrida has stressed in *Positions* the political effectiveness of inverting binary oppositions, of inversion as a stage in displacement.[7] The force of these arguments, both of which are complex and which I can only allude to here[8] but whose importance I want to stress, increases if we observe further the extent to which binarism produces an instability in the very process of categorically dividing the world. It both produces ambiguities which it can't contain and invites transgression in and of its own terms. Thus the opposition us/them produces the scandal of the internal dissident; the opposition masculine/feminine produces the scandal of the transvestite, not to mention the troubling ambiguity of the hermaphrodite.

For my purposes here, the most interesting and relevant senses of "inversion" and "perversion" are not primarily or specifically sexual. Traditionally inversion could mean reversal of position and reversal of direction, both being inimical to effective government and social stability. This sense of *active* alteration is there even more strikingly in perversion. Especially interesting is the slippage in an *OED* definition from divergence to evil: "turned away from the right way or from what is right or good; perverted, wicked"; similarly with another definition: "not in accordance with the accepted practice; incorrect, wrong." It is in this sense of actively altering—a divergence which is also a turning back upon—that the female transvestite of the early seventeenth century could be described as an "invert" and not at all in the sense of that word coined and popularized by the nineteenth-century sexologists (e.g., Krafft-Ebing and Havelock Ellis).

III

The female transvestite was indeed a deeply disturbing figure in the early seventeenth century.[9] As Lisa Jardine has recently reminded us, nowhere was the tension and struggle between classes, between residual and emergent cultures, between the mercantile order and what it was actually, or seemed to be, replacing, between rank and wealth, more apparent than in the obsession with dress and what it signified socially (141–42, 150).[10] Hence the attacks on the dress violations of the emergent (middle) class and the insubordinate (female) sex. The ideology of gender difference was just as fundamental as that of class in securing the social order. In fact patriarchy, class, and hierarchy all presupposed a law of gender difference which was at once divinely, naturally, and socially laid down, the law descending from the first through the second to the third.

It is *against and (again) in terms of* this metaphysic that dress violation occurred. A significant focus for the controversy was, of course, the theater, which, like the transvestite, was seen both to epitomize and promote contemporary forces of disruption. There was, for example, the general cultural disturbance generated by the theatrical emphasis on artifice, disguise, and role playing. Its significance can be gauged in part by looking at the range of objections to the theater as a place which subverted metaphysical fixity.

To begin with, the players were seen to undermine the idea that one's identity and place were a function of what one essentially was—what God had made one. The idea of a God-given nature and destiny had the corollary that nothing so essentially predetermined could or should ever change. In the words of one satirist, it was not so much that the player disguised his real self in playing; rather he had no self apart from that which he was playing: "The Statute hath done wisely to acknowledge him a Rogue and errant, for his chiefe essence is, *A daily Counterfeit* . . . His {profession} is compounded of all Natures, all humours, all professions."[11] The association here of the player and the rogue is significant. Both were itinerants and masterless men, sometimes both subjected to the same vagrancy laws (alternatively the player might be a royal servant—an interesting opposition in itself). They transgressed fixity not only because they were without fixed abode, but also because they lacked the identity which, in a hierarchical society, was essentially conferred by one's place in that society. But there was a further link among rogues, masterless men, and the players; according to some observers the theaters quite literally brought them into association, being the place "for vagrant persons, Masterless men, thieves, . . . contrivers of treason, and other idle and dangerous persons to meet together" (Chambers 4:122). Again we see the same anxiety: social stability depended crucially on people staying just as they were (identity), where they were (location), and doing what they always had done (calling). When the rogue meets the player two lawless identities converge.

This concern with unfixed identity was not unique to the theater; society and politics more generally contained a theatrical dimension, what Greenblatt calls "the theatricalisation of culture." Renaissance courts involved theatricality "in the sense of both disguise and histrionic self-presentation," while court manuals and rhetorical handbooks offered "an integrated rhetoric of the self, a model for the formation of an artificial identity" (162). And dissimulation was of course essential for the practice of realpolitik. The theater, then, provided a model, indeed a sustained exploration, of the role playing which was so important for social mobility, the appropriation and successful deployment of power. It follows that the recurring emphasis within Elizabethan and Jacobean plays on life itself as a process of playing was not merely theatrical projection; the world as a stage, life as artifice: these were ideas which the theater derived from as well as conveyed to its culture. As Louis Montrose has pointed out, this has a fascinating consequence: "If the world is a theatre and the theatre is an image of the world, then by reflecting upon its own artifice, the drama is holding the mirror up to nature" (57).

Another, related, charge against the players is that in their dress violations they—again like the "street" transvestites—transgressed the natural and fixed order of things by willfully confusing categories which it was thought imperative should be kept distinct, especially within the categories of gender, rank, and class. Boys playing women, menials playing those of a higher rank and breeding—to some these actions seemed deep violations of the principle of fixed division on which civilization rested. In Act 5, scene 5, of *Volpone* Mosca enters dressed as a gentleman:

> MOSCA
> But what am I?
>
> VOLPONE
> 'Fore heav'n, a brave *clarissimo*; thou becomest it!
> Pity thou wert not born one.
>
> MOSCA
>   If I hold
> My made one, 'twill be well.
>
> (5.5.2–5)

Mosca prevaricates beautifully. It's a reply which is at once deferential and contemptuous, self-effacing and arrogant. 'Twill be well because he is not the real thing, never could be, and isn't now even presuming; but conversely, 'twill be well because the imitation, the travesty of the real thing can also usurp it and to all intents and purposes become it. What price, then, that metaphysical guarantee of social differentiation when it is so easily abolished in the confusion it was supposed to preempt and render impossible? It is a moment of concentrated ambiguity, of irony (irony and ambiguity tend to be intrinsic to transgressive reinscription and alien to humanist transgression). It is also a moment of appropriation in which there surfaces the play's underlying knowledge, at once (for Jonson) exhilarating, ambivalent, appalling, and violent; a knowledge which incites yet also fears that riot of the perverse, the antisocial, and the antinatural which are *Volpone*.

One further aspect of dress violation associated with the theater also contravened divine and natural law: the abomination of boys dressing as girls. For John Rainolds the boy transvestite destroyed the fragile moral restraint containing an anarchic male sexuality; the boy incited his male audience into every kind of perversion, mostly homosexual, but heterosexual too. Rainolds saw adult male sexuality not just as anarchic but as satanically polymorphous, seemingly capable of attaching to the forbidden with alarming ease.[12] Rainolds apart, the transgressions associated with the boy players, be they actual or imagined, rendered the theatrical self-consciousness surrounding transvestism complex and shifting; it provoked questions which were teasingly unanswerable: for example—and this is a question especially intriguing for us today—which, or how many, of the several gender identities embodied in any one figure are in play at any one time?

IV

In *The Roaring Girl* (1608–11), a play with a transvestite hero/ine and in the 1620 pamphlet controversy over cross-dressing, which treated issues similar to those in the play, the contemporary sexual metaphysic was turned inside out: gender division was recognized as central not to a divinely sanctioned natural order but to a contingent and oppressive social order. Correspondingly the representation of gender inversion generates an interrogation of both the sexual metaphysic and the social order. Moll Cutpurse, the transvestite hero/ine of

The Roaring Girl, is variously described as one who "strays so from her kind / Nature repents she made her" (1.2.211–20); who some say "is a man / And some both man and woman" (2.1.190–91), and yet others that she is "a codpiece-daughter" (2.2.89):

> a thing
> One knows not how to name: her birth began
> Ere she was all made: 'tis woman more than man,
> Man more than woman, and (*which to none can hap*)
> The sun gives her two shadows to one shape
>   (1.2.128–32; italics added)

And yet this creature who so violates the natural order and traditional gender divisions by dressing as a man also does things better than a man: "I should draw first and prove the quicker man," she says (4.1.76)—and she does. In the process she attacks masculinity as a charade, asserting its failure *in its own sexual terms* (2.9.290 ff.), something which the language of the play echoes elsewhere, facetiously, but defensively, too (cf. 2.1.326 ff.; 2.2.75 ff.; 3.1.142 ff.). Moll also offers the truly exceptional view of prostitution as a sexual exploitation rooted in economic exploitation and patriarchal power:

> In thee I defy all men, their worst hates,
> And their best flatteries, all their golden witchcrafts,
> With which they entangle the poor spirits of fools.
> Distressed needlewomen and trade-fallen wives,
> Fish that must needs bite or themselves be bitten,
> Such hungry things as these may soon be took
> With a worm fastened on a golden hook:
> Those are the lecher's food, his prey, he watches
> For quarrelling wedlocks, and poor shifting sisters.
>   (3.1.90–98)[13]

Recognizing all this, and being shown, too, where the power lies in this social order, the politics of inversion become persuasive, perhaps irresistible; this is Moll, about to thrash the predatory Laxton: "I scorn to prostitute myself to a man, / I that can prostitute a man to me" (3.1.109–10). Moll's denunciation of Laxton before she beats him up shows that the thrashing is partly in revenge for his not untypical masculine blend of misogyny and promiscuity (cf. 2.2.252–55), to which of course the prostitute can indeed testify (and perhaps also confirm): if these things appear incompatible—isn't misogyny a kind of hatred, and promiscuity a kind of love, albeit a debased one?—in reality they go hand in hand.

It's in these ways that *The Roaring Girl* begins to disclose how, because of the complex connections between sexuality, gender, and class, between sexual and economic exploitation, economic and political anxieties can be displaced into the domain of the sexual and, conversely, the sexual comes to possess enormous signifying power. Indeed, the king himself intervened in 1620 to try to eliminate female transvestitism.[14] He, like many others at that time, felt female transvestites were usurping male authority. This is indeed exactly what Moll does throughout the play, and especially when she beats up Laxton. But perhaps more importantly the transvestite was contributing to a knowledge and a culture which undermined the discursive formations of authority itself, through her perverse reinscription within those formations. This can be further illustrated, briefly, from the pamphlet controversy.

Hic Mulier, the voice of female transvestites in the most interesting pamphlet, *Haec Vir* (1620), insists that gender difference is an effect of custom only. Custom becomes the cause where once it was only the effect. Again, inversion. This is also an instance of what was to become the classic move in ideological demystification: the metaphysical is first displaced by, and then collapsed into, the social. Shorn of its metaphysical sanction, law, especially in the Renaissance, is in danger of losing its prescriptive power. Nothing is more absurd, nothing more foolish, says Hic Mulier, than custom. In fact, it is "an idiot" (Sig.B2; spelling modernized). The radical implications of this assertion can be seen from an observation of Montaigne's: "We may easily discern, that only custom makes that seem impossible unto us, which is not so" (1:39). Throughout the pamphlet Hic Mulier seems to be in sympathy with this remark of Montaigne's, but nowhere is her appropriation of the idea more challenging than in the way she dissolves both law and ideological fixity into a celebration of change and transformation and, by implication, a celebration of her potential rather than her fixed nature: "Nor do I in my delight of change otherwise than as the whole world does" (Sig.B). At a time when many thought of change as synonymous with evil, or at least decline and degeneracy, this was indeed provocative. Hic Mulier is not only shameless but, as Sandra Clark has recently pointed out, she suggests that shame itself "is a concept framed by men to subordinate women to the dictates of arbitrary custom" (175). Hic Mulier claims, too, that women are as reasonable as men. And then the crucial claim: "We are as free born as men, have as free election, and as free spirits; we are compounded of like parts, and may with like liberty make benefit of our creations" (Sig.B3). It's a claim whose force in *this* instance comes through a demystification generated across inversion.

But consider now a misgiving voiced by Linda Woodbridge and shared by many others: "To me the one unsatisfying feature of the otherwise stimulating transvestite movement is that it had to be transvestite: Renaissance women so far accepted the masculine rules of the game that they felt they had to look masculine to be free" (145). For understandable reasons Woodbridge seems to prefer the "hermaphroditic vision" (145 and cf.317). The transvestite and the hermaphrodite: both were disturbing images; perhaps they are less so now. Potentially the hermaphrodite dissolves gender difference and, at least in its associated idea of androgyny, has become acceptable. Even in the Renaissance the figure could "symbolise the essential oneness of the sexes" (Woodbridge 140), and, with reference back to Plato's *Symposium*, the recovery of an original lost unity (itself intrinsically sexual). The idea remains alive today, of course; Kaja Silverman reminds us that the notion of an original androgynous whole, similar to that projected by Aristophanes, is absolutely central to the psychoanalytic theories of Jacques Lacan, where the human subject is defined in terms of an essential, intrinsic lack, because it is believed to be a fragment of something larger and more primordial (152–53). But the transvestite? S/he is a strange and disturbing figure still, though for different reasons now than in the Renaissance. Isn't s/he a figure who has exchanged one kind of incompleteness for another? If misgivings persist they are not exactly moral; I mean we don't exactly or openly disapprove. Isn't it rather that, as Woodbridge implies, the transvestite seems to be a victim of false consciousness, and by switching gender roles rather than dissolving them, reinforces the very sexual division which s/he finds oppressive? In this view the transvestite fails the test of humanist transgression, a perspective which pervades literary criticism still. But if the hermaphrodite threatens the binarism of gender through ambiguous unity, the female transvestite of the early seventeenth century positively disrupts that same scheme by usurping the master side of the opposition. To invoke again the earlier distinction between different kinds of transgression, the transvestite represents a subversive reinscription within, rather than a transcendence of, an existing order, while the hermaphrodite is often appropriated as a symbol of just such a transcendence. Essentially the aggressive female cross-dresser inverted the metaphysics of difference: from being a divine law inscribed essentially in each of God's subjects, which knowledge of self would confirm, sexual identity (and difference) is shifted irretreivably into the domain of custom, of the social, of that which can be contested. Perhaps this is the mode of transgression denied to the hermaphrodite, at least when associated with the mythological, the presocial, the transcendent.

V

What I've just offered have been partial readings of the *Haec Vir* pamphlet and *The Roaring Girl*, partial not in the sense (at least this isn't what I'm confessing) of being distortions of the texts, but rather readings that focus upon textual elements which can be correlated with oppositional cultural elements within Jacobean society, and consequently possible audience positions and reading responses. But the representation of the transvestite in the pamphlet and the theater is part of a cultural process whose complexity is worth exploring further. The complexity I'm concerned with isn't that supposed intrinsic property of the text which politically motivated critics always distort (in biased readings) and impartial critics transparently represent (in long readings). It's the complexity which is first and foremost a social process, and within which the text was, and still is, implicated. Viewing the text as part of a social process raises, unavoidably, the question of the containment of transgression. Both play and pamphlet have been seen to move toward a closure which contains—even eradicates—their challenging elements.

The *Haec-Vir* pamphlet ends, notoriously, with Hic Mulier declaring that women like her have only become masculine because men have become effeminate. They have taken up men's cast-off garments in order to "support a difference"(Sig. C2V)—in effect to maintain a sexual difference being abandoned by men. And if men revert to being masculine, the Hic Mulier figure continues, women will once again become feminine *and* subordinate. Actually this conclusion barely constitutes containment. To see this argument as somehow cancelling what went before is probably to interpret the pamphlet according to inappropriate notions of authorial intention, character utterance, and textual unity (all three notions privileging what is said finally as being more truthful than what went before). The Hic Mulier figure (an abstraction) is a vehicle for a variety of defenses of the transvestite, radical *and* conservative, and there is no good reason, given the genre, to privilege the one over the others as more truthful, more sincere, more representative, or to be dismayed that some of these arguments are incompatible with each other. Presumably, if the different defenses had been split between several Hic Mulier figures the problem (for us) would disappear—again alerting us to certain, not necessarily appropriate, interpretative assumptions. But it is also true that this culminating defense, conservative as it is, still partakes of the same fundamental challenge to gender division as the other defenses: to suggest that gender difference can be maintained through cross-dressing and inversion is still to maintain or imply the crucial claim: it is difference working in terms of custom and culture (and so contestable) rather than nature and divine law (and so immutable). Even with this conservative (ironic?) defense, then, sexual difference is sustained by the very inversion which divine law forbids, and the fact that it can be so sustained is simultaneously a repudiation of the claim that sexual difference is itself dictated by divine or natural law.

The Roaring Girl is a much more interesting instance of containment. Right at the outset we're alerted to the fact that Mary Frith, the real-life cross-dresser on whom the play is based, is being given a more virtuous image than she in fact possessed (Dedication 19 ff.; Prologue 26–27). The play plays down Frith's criminality. She seems to have been several times arrested and variously recorded as being a bawd, thief, receiver, gang leader, and whore, all of which, as Andor Gomme remarks, the character Moll Cutpurse definitely is not, and is only falsely accused of being in the play.[15] Whereas the deviance of Mary Frith remained in certain respects implacably immoral and antisocial, in the figure of Moll Cutpurse she is remade as the moral conscience of the selfsame society whose gender categories she transgresses. More specifically, Frith/Moll is appropriated for a partial critique of patriarchal law, sexual exploitation, and aristocratic culture. At the same time she remains "isolated from the very social structure which her courage and vitality have done so much to enliven and renew" (Rose 389–90). In this respect Frith/Moll is represented in the tradition of the warrior woman and the folk figure of Long Meg of Westminster, both of whom distinguish true morality from false, the proper man from the braggart, and finally submit to the former (see Shepherd esp. 70–72). At the same time, Moll, a figure who epitomizes the abnormal and the degenerate, and who also apparently incites lewdness in others, paradoxically helps regenerate a degenerate society and especially its ailing patriarchal basis: "Moll: Father and son, I ha' done you simple service here" (5.2.206). Thus the relationship between the dominant and the deviant is nothing if not complex: if the demonizing of the deviant other leads to suppression and even extermination, the colonizing of the (internal) deviant involves an assimilation which re-forms, ethically and literally, even as it re-presents. The play reconstitutes Mary Frith as Moll Cutpurse, who in turn is used to reconstitute a social order while remaining on its margins—reformed and reforming but not finally incorporated; hence Moll's parting injunction to the assembled "gentlemen" of the final scene, "I pursue no pity: / Follow the law" (252–55).

In this case containment isn't the reaction of power after, and in response to, the event of subversion. It's intrinsic to the process of literary representation, social contest, and social change. Perhaps, then, containment is best seen as always already in play, even before we can identify a dominant-subversive opposition, or indeed anything like a subversive event. But by the same token, containment can effect rather than defeat change (and this doesn't presuppose the desirability or otherwise of that change; it might be reaction or progress or, as in this play, complex elements of both with each differently appropriated for different audience positions). Rather than seeing containment as that which preempts and defeats transgression we need to see both as potentially productive processes. *The Roaring Girl* presents a process in which containment of the deviant forms the basis of one social faction offering a critique of, and taking power from, another. In a more radical dynamic, containment, in the very process of repressing one kind of subversive knowledge, actually produces another. It is to the latter process that I now turn.

VI

Perhaps the most interesting theatrical containment of the transvestite challenge occurs in Fletcher's *Love's Cure* (1624?).[16] Indeed, one wonders if the play was written as a conservative response to the controversy, since it directly addresses the most challenging claim or implication of the radical transvestite, namely, that gender division and inequality are a consequence not of divine or natural law but of social custom. The play centers on the severe cultural disturbance generated by the fact that Clara, a girl, has been brought up as a boy and wants to remain one, while her brother, Lucio, has been brought up as a girl, which he wants to remain, despite the fact that society is now demanding that both return to their normal gender ascriptions. It's a humorous situation and one played up as such. But the play also acknowledges that what is at stake is nothing less than the legitimacy of the whole social order, hinging as it does on a "naturally" sanctioned law of sexual difference. This is a play about the perversion of nature by culture (or "custom"—1.2.47, 2.2.95–97) with the eventual triumph of nature: "Nature (though long kept back) wil have her owne" (4.4.61–62; cf.2.2.248–59, 4.2.187–90, 5.3.90–94).

The cultural conditioning of both Lucio and Clara seems to go deep. Parents and others try yet fail to restore the children to their natural selves; the father, Alvarez, cries angrily:

> Can strong habituall custome
> Work with such Magick on the mind, and manners
> In spight of sex and nature?
>
> (2.2.140–42)

The answer is, apparently, yes. But then nature succeeds where authority has failed; attraction to the opposite sex awakens the siblings' own "true" natural instincts, and gender incongruities are resolved.

Clara switches from being aggressive to being acquiescent, and Lucio does the reverse. Right order prevails.

We might say that *Love's Cure* produces transgression precisely in order to contain it, and in the most insidiously ideological way: desire which initially appeared to contradict nature is reconstituted by nature in accord with her (?) order. Reconstituted, not repressed: desire itself is transformed, not coerced, back from the perverse to the natural. But in the process the very masculine code of honor which is affronted by Lucio's perverse failure of masculinity is shown to border on a perversity even more excessive than his. It is as if containment, in reinstating nature over culture—that most fundamental and violent of binary oppositions—protests too much about both. Thus the strategy of containment resembles the unintended power of the subordinates who execute the commands of the powerful and of whom the Governor complains:

> How men in high place, and authority
> Are in their lives and estimation wrong'd
> By their subordinate Ministers? *yet such*
> *They cannot but imploy.*
>
> (4.3.119–22; emphasis added)

Masculine sexuality is shown to be complex and unstably implicated within the whole social domain. Either nature doesn't contain it or nature contains too much to be conceived any longer as natural. What is especially fascinating about this text is that a relegitimation of masculinity coexists with an ironic critique of it, and a representation of masculinity's cultural unconscious. An urbane text, it nevertheless discloses a violent scenario—social, psychic, and sexual (what has sometimes been mistaken for decadence).

Most obviously and consciously there is the fact that Lucio's effeminacy, construed by Bobadillo as an affront to "heav'n, and nature, and thy Parents" (2.2.22)—i.e., divine, natural, and patriarchal law—actually involves positive civilized virtues. Lucio would, for example, willingly renounce the savage illogic whereby a bloody family feud is being perpetuated (2.2.44 ff.) and also the sword as instrument and symbol of male violence (2.4.84 ff.). And then his father, raging at Lucio's inability to become a "real" man, demands final proof of his masculinity: he must attack the very next man he sees and sexually assault the first woman (4.3.37 ff.). Though conceived as an absolute, uncompromising ethical stand ("Life's but a word, a shadow, a melting dreame, / Compar'd to essentiall, and eternall honour"—5.3.124–25), masculine honor is also represented as barbaric. Two of its basic characteristics are sexual prowess and violence, and they are inextricably related, as indicated for example by the conventional but still revealingly obsessive association of sword and phallus (e.g., at 2.2.86–90 and 5.3.194–96) and the ambiguity of "blood," at once sexual desire and what honor demands, literally, of the male opponent.

From such punning we see that masculine sexuality is confirmed not only by women, passively, but also actively by other men. Actively: it isn't so much that the culture of masculine honor is a sublimation of homosexuality; rather it repeatedly incites what heterosexually it cannot admit. The differential status of men and women in confirming masculine sexuality is neatly demonstrated at the climax of the play, the arranged duel between Alvarez and Vitelli (seconded, respectively, by the now masculine Lucio and Lamorall). As they square up to each other the spouses of the first three men "*Enter above*" and implore them not to fight. Plea after plea fails. "Are you men, or stone," cries the Governor; "Men, and we'l prove it with our swords" replies Alvarez (5.3.172–73). And what honor dictates must take place between men—alliance/violence—simply overrides honorable vows to women (162–64). In fact the women's pleas for peace only intensify the men's desire to fight. Within masculine sexuality the most significant other is the male—but it is a significance which still presupposes the female. Thus when the women threaten to kill themselves it's as if the currents of sexuality and violence, circulating between the men and sustaining sexual difference between male and female, are suddenly switched off; the threatened self-annihilation of the women is also a threatened breaking of the circuit. If they die the most necessary spectators and objects of masculine performance disappear. Also, in this *reductio ad absurdum* of masculine sexuality, men become redundant as the women threaten to perform phallic violence on themselves in order to forestall male violence (Genevora to the duelists: "The first blow given betwixt you, sheathes these swords / In one anothers bosomes" [177–78]).

Masculinity is rooted in a sexual violence performed inseparably against both men and women. Vitelli to Clara:

> When on this point, I have pearch'd thy father's soule.
> Ile tender thee this bloody reeking hand
> Drawne forth the bowels of that murtherer:
> If thou canst love me then, I'le marry thee.
> And for thy father lost, get thee a Sonne;
> On no condition else.
>
> (104–09)

In the reiterated pun, sword and phallus substitute for each other. But here we might read/see something more: Vitelli's violence against Clara's father is erotically identified with the sexual act performed "with" her. Vitelli will kill her father and replace him with a son born of her. It's the supreme narcissistic displacement of the rival male via the very woman whom each struggles to possess. Further, this promised birth will implicate Clara in Vitelli's violence without at all changing her status as its abject victim. And the violence against her father is as sexual as the proposed sexual intercourse "with" Clara is violent. Vitelli doubly substitutes himself for Clara's father: first as her husband, then as himself in her son.

This incident is not the first time that Vitelli has insisted to Clara that his sexual desire for her is conjoined with an equally strong desire to kill her father and brother:

> He, whose tongue thus gratifies the daughter,
> And sister of his enemy, weares a Sword
> To rip the father and the brother up.
> . . . .
> That my affections should promiscuously
> Dart love and hate at once, both worthily!
>
> (2.2.189–95)

Speaking of himself in the second person Vitelli presents masculine desire as spectacle, again narcissistically demanding confirmation of an audience even as he also conceives his masculinity as spontaneous, autonomous desire.

The opposite of honorable antagonism is honorable alliance, affirmed in the image and name of the brother. But what are in one sense dramatically opposed kinds of relationships are in another simply alternative celebrations of masculinity. Elsewhere in Beaumont and Fletcher's work valorous males similarly oscillate between honorable antagonism and honorable alliance, in an almost erotic state of arousal. In both kinds of relationship men recognize and reinforce each other's sexuality in the triangle man-man-woman. But even as they enter into relations of honorable alliance it is with an unspoken understanding: "I don't desire you; I desire to be like you." This repeated disavowal of direct desire in favor of imitative alliance is a crucial precondition of one kind of male bonding (what someone once called penises in parallel).

Frequently in this period the representation of the triangle suggests that the desire which bonds men over women is as erotically invested for the men in relation to each other as for each of them in relation to the women. In *The Maid's Tragedy*, Melantius, approving his sister's marriage to his best friend, tells her: "Sister, I joy to see you, and your choice. / You look'd with my eyes when you took that man" (*The Maid's Tragedy* 1.2.107–08). Another revealing recurrence in Jacobean plays is the way that male sexual jealousy, even as it is represented as obsessively heterosexual in its demands, produces eroticized images of the rival male simultaneously with the denigration of the woman:

> FERDINAND
>   my imagination will carry me
> To see her in the shameful act of sin
> . . . .
> Happily, with some strong thigh'd bargeman;
> Or one o'th' wood-yard, that can quoit the sledge
> Or toss the bar, or else some lovely squire
> That carries coals up to her privy lodgings.
> . . . .
>   Go to, mistress!
> 'Tis not your whore's milk that shall quench my wildfire,
> But your whore's blood.
>   (2.5.40–49)

In *The Maid's Tragedy*, when the King becomes sexually jealous of Amintor, he too evokes his rival in terms which eroticize him, showing again that the cult of masculine honor circulating in this court is ineradicably erotic (3.1).

Seemingly, masculine identity always requires masculine ratification, but in the process is potentially complicated by a homoerotic desire in the very situations in which heterosexuality is most ardently pursued. It's as if, with so much mutual admiration about, some of it just cannot help but transform into deviant desire for, rather than honorable imitation of, "man's" most significant other (i.e., man). But should we call this dynamic homoerotic? It certainly is erotic, but perhaps it is better described, following Eve Sedgwick,[17] as homosocial desire, if only to avoid erroneous assumptions about its origin and "nature." For example, it seems to me that this process does not necessarily involve the irruption of repressed homosexual desire as conceived by Freud;[18] rather it is the eroticizing of a bond, an eroticism largely preconditioned by the social intensity of that bond.

To shift in this analysis from the transvestite to the issue of masculine sexuality is only to follow one trajectory of transvestism itself during this period: in appropriating, inverting, and substituting for masculinity, the female transvestite inevitably put masculinity itself—and sexual difference more generally—under scrutiny. Further, in the attempted containment of transvestism (*Love's Cure*) masculinity and sexual difference are put in question in a different way; in the control of one hostile knowledge another is inadvertently produced; suppression of an (in)subordinate deviance discloses other, equally disturbing deviations at the heart of the dominant, homoerotic deviations whose repression is a condition of domination in one of its important forms: homosocial male bonding. Finally, the transvestite challenge to masculinity and sexual difference works in terms of transgressive inversion and reinscription, not of transcendence or the recovery of authentic selfhood. We are as free born as men, says the Hic Mulier figure, and she says it in drag. Not so much knowing thyself, then, as knowing thy discursive formations—knowing them in the process of living but also inverting them; reinscribing oneself within, succumbing to, dis-locating, demystifying them.

Notes

¹For further analysis of custom in this respect see Dollimore, esp. 9–19.

²See also Crompton.

³Anthropological and historical studies of inversion in the Renaissance have stressed both its ubiquity and its cultural significance. But what and how it signified—in particular whether it disrupted or ratified those dominant forms being inverted—depended crucially on context and cannot be decided independently of it. See especially Davis, and Kunzle, both in Babcock; and Stallybrass and White.

⁴See Davis, and Kunzle.

⁵Cf. Freud: "defiance signifies dependence *as much as obedience does,* though with a 'minus' instead of a 'plus' sign before it" *(Introductory Lectures on Psychoanalysis* 495; emphasis added).

⁶Freud's noted instance of the return of the repressed also involves the Crucifixion. In an etching by Félicien Rops an ascetic monk looks to the Crucifixion to banish his own temptation, but in place of Christ he sees "the image of a voluptuous, naked woman, in the same crucified attitude. . . . Rops has placed Sin in the very place of the Saviour on the cross. He seems to have known that, when what has been repressed returns, it emerges from the repressing force itself." Freud, *Art and Literature* 60.

⁷Derrida 41–42. Derrida stresses the importance of inversion as a stage in the process of displacing the binary. Even with this formulation it is easy to overlook the extent to which, in actual practice, in historical reality, an inversion already achieves a degree of displacement.

⁸I explore this further in a related article, "The Dominant and the Deviant."

⁹This section is indebted to and was inspired by a number of recent studies of the transvestite controversy, especially the following: Dusinberre, esp. 231–305; Shepherd, esp. ch. 6; Jardine, esp. ch. 5; Woodbridge, esp. part 2; Rose, 367–91; Clark 157–83.

¹⁰See also Whigham 155–69.

¹¹"A Common Player," 1615, quoted from Montrose 51 and 57.

¹²*Overthrow of Stage-Plays, 1599.* See also Binns 95–120; Jardine, ch. 1.

¹³See also Woodbridge 254–55.

¹⁴See Chamberlain 2: 286–89.

¹⁵Gomme, xiv; see also Shepherd 74–76.

¹⁶All quotations from *Love's Cure* are from the Williams edition. A much-needed single-volume edition of this text is in preparation by J. Marea Mitchell for the Nottingham Drama Texts Series, ed. George Parfitt et al. Mitchell also analyzes the play in her dissertation, "Gender and Identity in Philip Sidney's *Arcadia.*" See also Shepherd, and Clark.

¹⁷Sedgwick, esp. Introduction and ch. 1; see also Girard.

¹⁸See for example Freud's description of this in his account of the Schreber case in *Case Histories II*, esp. 199–200.

Works Cited

BABCOCK, BARBARA A. *The Reversible World: Symbolic Inversion in Art and Society*. Ithaca and London: Cornell UP, 1978.

BEAUMONT, F., and FLETCHER, J. *The Maid's Tragedy*. Ed. H. B. Norland. Regents Renaissance Drama Series. London: Arnold, 1968.

BINNS, J. W. "Women or Transvestites on the Elizabethan Stage?: An Oxford Controversy." *Sixteenth Century Journal* 5 (1974): 95–120.

BROWN, RITA MAE. *Rubyfruit Jungle*. London: Corgi, 1978.

CHAMBERLAIN, JOHN. *Letters*. Ed. Norman E. McClure. 2 vols. Philadelphia: American Philosophical Society, 1939.

CHAMBERS, E. K. *The Elizabethan Stage*. 4 vols. Oxford: Clarendon, 1923.

CLARK, SANDRA. "*Hic Mulier, Haec Vir*, and the Controversy over Masculine Women." *Studies in Philology* 82 (Spring 1985): 157–83.

CROMPTON, LOUIS. "The Myth of Lesbian Impunity: Capital Laws from 1270–1791." *Journal of Homosexuality* 6 (1980–81): 11–25.

DAVIES, SIR JOHN. *Nosce Teipsum. Poems*. Ed. Robert Krueger. Oxford: Clarendon, 1975.

DAVIS, NATALIE ZEMON. "Women on Top: Symbolic Sexual Inversion and Political Disorder in Early Modern Europe." *The Reversible World: Symbolic Inversion in Art and Society*. Ithaca and London: Cornell UP, 1978.

DERRIDA, JACQUES. *Positions*. London: Athlone, 1981.

DOLLIMORE, JONATHAN. *Radical Tragedy*. Brighton: Harvester, 1984; Chicago: U of Chicago P, 1984.

———. "The Dominant and the Deviant: A Violent Dialectic." *Critical Quarterly* 28 (1986).

DUSINBERRE, JULIET. *Shakespeare and the Nature of Women*. London: Macmillan, 1975.

FADERMAN, LILLIAN. *Surpassing the Love of Men: Romantic Friendship and Love between Women from the Renaissance to the Present*. London: Dent, 1981.

FLETCHER, JOHN. *The Dramatic Works in the Beaumont and Fletcher Canon*. Ed. George W. Williams. Gen. ed. Fredson Bowers. Vol. 3. Cambridge: Cambridge UP, 1976.

FOUCAULT, MICHAEL. *The History of Sexuality*. Vol. 1: *An Introduction*. New York: Vintage, 1980.

FREUD, SIGMUND. *Case Histories II*. The Pelican Freud Library 9. Harmondsworth: Pelican Books, 1979.

_____. *Introductory Lectures on Psychoanalysis*. The Pelican Freud Library 1. Harmondsworth: Pelican Books, 1976.

_____. *Art and Literature*. The Pelican Freud Library 14. Harmondsworth: Pelican Books, 1985.

GIDE, ANDRÉ. *The Immoralist*. Harmondsworth: Penguin, 1960.

GIRARD, RENÉ. *Deceit, Desire and the Novel: Self and Others in Literary Structure*. Baltimore: Johns Hopkins UP, 1965.

GOMME, ANDOR. Introduction. *The Roaring Girl*. By Middleton and Dekker. London: Benn, 1976.

GREENBLATT, STEPHEN. *Renaissance Self-Fashioning*. Chicago: U of Chicago P, 1980.

Hic Mulier: Or, the Man-Woman and *Haec-Vir: Or, the Womanish-Man*. 1620. The University of Essex: The Rota, 1973.

HOOKER, RICHARD. *Of the Laws of Ecclesiastical Polity*. 2 vols. London: Dent, 1969.

JARDINE, LISA. *Still Harping on Daughters: Women and Drama in the Age of Shakespeare*. Brighton: Harvester, 1983.

KUNZLE, DAVID. "World Turned Upside Down: The Iconography of a European Broadsheet Type." Babcock.

MIDDLETON, THOMAS, and THOMAS DEKKER, *The Roaring Girl*. The New Mermaid edition. Ed. A. Gomme. London: Benn, 1976.

MITCHELL, J. MAREA. "Gender and Identity in Philip Sidney's *Arcadia*." Diss. U of Sussex, 1985.

MONTAIGNE, MICHEL. *Essays*. Trans. John Florio. 3 vols. London: Dent, 1965.

MONTROSE, LOUIS. 'The Purpose of Playing: Reflections on a Shakespearean Anthropology." *Helios* ns 7 (1980): 51–74.

NEWTON, ESTHER. "The Mythic Mannish Lesbian: Radclyffe Hall and the New Woman." *The Lesbian Issue: Essays from Signs*. Ed. Estelle B. Freeman et al. Chicago: U of Chicago P, 1985.

RAINOLDS, JOHN. *Overthrow of Stage-Plays.* 1599. Theatrum Redividium Series. New York, 1972.

ROSE, MARY BETH. "Women in Men's Clothing: Apparel and Social Stability in *The Roaring Girl.*" *English Literary Renaissance* 14 (1984): 367–91.

SALGÁDO, G., ed. *Cony-Catchers and Bawdy Baskets.* Penguin English Library. Harmondsworth, 1972.

SEDGWICK, EVE KOSOFSKY. *Between Men: English Literature and Male Homosocial Desire.* New York: Columbia UP, 1985.

SENNETT, RICHARD. *Authority.* London: Secker, 1980.

SHEPHERD, SIMON. *Amazons and Warrior Women: Varieties of Feminism in Seventeenth-Century Drama.* Brighton: Harvester, 1981.

SILVERMAN, KAJA. *The Subject of Semiotics.* New York: Oxford UP, 1983.

STALLYBRASS, PETER, and ALLON WHITE. *The Politics and Poetics of Transgression.* London: Methuen, 1986.

WEBSTER, JOHN. *The Duchess of Malfi. Selected Plays.* Ed. Jonathan Dollimore and Alan Sinfield. Cambridge: Cambridge UP, 1983.

WHIGHAM, FRANK. *Ambition and Privilege: The Social Tropes of Elizabethan Courtesy Theory.* Berkeley: U of California P, 1984.

WOODBRIDGE, LINDA. *Women and the English Renaissance: Literature and the Nature of Womankind,* 1540–1620. Brighton: Harvester, 1984; Urbana: U of Illinois P, 1984.

Way Stations in the Errancy of the Word: A Study of Calderón's La vida es sueño

RUTH EL SAFFAR

IN ANSWER to Derrida's assessment of the written word's nature as "coupée de toute responsabilité absolue, de la *conscience* comme autorité de dernière instance, orphaline et separée dès sa naissance de l'assistance de son père" (Derrida's emphasis), Thomas Greene in *The Light in Troy* restores meaning to the word by anchoring it—albeit temporarily—in a series of more or less nurturing contexts.[1] For Greene *écriture* is not so much a "Dickensian child-hero" as an entity acquiring "a kind of ubiquitous foster parent in the presence of the maternal culture that has adopted it" (16). Though neither Greene nor Derrida underscores it—in fact, *because* neither underscores it—their respective metaphors regarding the written word's fate provide interesting commentary on the unconscious ground out of which their speculations arise. Derrida's written word is severed from any absolute responsibility, and from consciousness as ultimate authority, because of its condition as "separée dès sa naissance de l'assistance de son *père*." Its hope for stability, for a responsible communal contribution, however, according to Greene, comes from the "*maternal* culture that has adopted it" (emphasis added).

The paternal and maternal metaphors—their unconscious association with authority and errancy on the one hand, and with nurture
and stability on the other—plunge us into what Greene calls a "communal intuition" (23) as long-standing as it has been, until very recently, inexpressible. Indeed, it is the nature of metaphor, as Greene later
points out so insightfully, to allude to the "intuitions of relationship
conceivable within a given culture" (22). Only now, with the perspective provided by recent efforts to understand the social and psychological effects of almost exclusively female parenting in early child-
hood are we in a position to bring to consciousness some part of the
nexus of associations that allows a writer to envision an ungrounded
word as both without consciousness and without paternity.[2] The unspoken metaphor in this case yokes responsibility and consciousness
with the presence of the father.[3] A less radical view of the nature of the
word, on the other hand, one that gives it temporary shelter against
the winds of chance and change, restores, through the maternal metaphor, the possibility of communication that Derrida's orphaned word
has lost. Greene's "maternal culture" links the notion of exchange and
interaction with the idea of mother.

Taken together, the two metaphors evoke primordial images of the
post-edenic nuclear family: the child (word) is abandoned by its father
(intention, consciousness), yet it is given by the mother (context) a
place in which, temporarily, to experience interaction. Derrida's challenge to the Western philosophical, logocentric tradition, which
Greene modifies but does not ultimately refuse, depends precisely on
the radical absence of the father. That absence, as we shall see in the
analysis of Calderón's *La vida es sueño* that follows here, opens up
language and culture, indeed, the whole notion of identity, to confrontation with the abyss. The acquisition of literacy brings alterity
with it, as Derrida so powerfully intuits (179–80). The sense of separation, absence, and fatherlessness that literacy brings as its necessary
complement, however, is exactly what it needs most to hide. Out of
the paternal void it will create, therefore, its own spectral authority,
an authority grounded, as Calderón saw only too clearly, on fear and
illusion, and having ultimately no referent beyond itself.

With the mass interiorization of the notion of language as *écriture*,
as that which is *written*, not spoken, Western culture in the sixteenth

century turned to the image not only of the word, but of the self as an entity separate from its environment.[4] The itinerary of the written word, whose description Derrida so persuasively offers, mirrors curiously that of Western culture, tracing out the solitary, fatherless wanderer in a culture given over since the Renaissance to the collective errancies of massive migrations—from farm to town, from native country to colonies. The written word, which allows for the first time—enforces, in fact—a separation between speaker and audience, between knower and known, spawned the fictions of the rogue and adventurer in a world that was throwing its sons and fathers in successive waves across oceans, into battle, and to universities away from home.

The condition of a written culture is that it identifies the self with the faculty of intellect, and must take toward the emotions and senses an attitude of distrust if not of outright hostility and rejection. The Cartesian *cogito* is a perfect philosophical representation of consciousness from the standpoint of written culture, just as *Lazarillo de Tormes* or *Robinson Crusoe* captures that culture in literature. What has tended to get lost, in this process of upheaval that the apotheosis of the intellect both fosters and reflects, is the sense of rootedness and culture that would ground either the flesh-and-blood wanderer or the errancies of the written word. It is with that issue that Greene and Derrida, using parental metaphors, continue to struggle.

In the *mundus* fomented in the Renaissance out of the collective phenomena of empire, conquest, large-scale education, and a print culture, the image of "father" elides with that of vagrant, abandoner, while "mother" becomes associated with charity, the foster home, the roadside inn. It should not come as a surprise that Spain would lead Western Europe in drawing out from the explosions of print, gunpowder, empire, and money in the sixteenth century the literary ramifications. *Lazarillo de Tormes* (1554) and *Don Quixote* Part I (1605) break, ahead of the rest of Western Europe, with the traditional literary forms to present characters, like their writers, at odds with their contexts, isolated, abandoned and abandoning, outside the order of patriarchy, and homeless. The novel, which so accurately images the effects of *écriture* on consciousness, develops first in that country in which separation, social upheaval, conquest, migration, and emigration are most deeply experienced by the populace. Both *Lazarillo de Tormes* and *Don Quixote*, while reflecting on the surface the crises of characters torn from the stabilities of home and an agriculturally based economy, also explore the limits of language: its distortions, its failures, and its capacity to confuse, mislead, and openly deceive. As will Derrida four centuries later, these texts reveal the written word's identity with rupture, absence, and instability.

The literary reaction to the slippage and rootlessness so accurately revealed in *Lazarillo de Tormes* and *Don Quixote* can be found in the scripts prepared—sometimes in as little as twenty-four hours—for the theaters that began as popular street performances in the 1580s and had moved, by the 1630s also into the sumptuous surroundings of the court. Both in its orientation toward the masses of citydwellers—often poor and illiterate—who flooded the urban centers from the countryside in the second half of the sixteenth century, and in its later turn toward the more refined audience of the court, the Spanish national theater affirmed the patriarchal order rendered so suspect in novels produced in the same period.

Walter Ong has noted that drama is—despite its oral delivery—the genre most thoroughly assimilated into the written culture.[5] As such, it is the genre most likely to affirm—in compensation—the paternity and maternity that the print culture tends by its very nature to destroy. In the Spanish *comedia* from the beginning the norms of father, king, and church are reinforced within a context premised on their erosion. The honoring of the rural, oral culture that Lope de Vega (1565–1635) evokes in so many of his early plays appeals to the nostalgia of an audience uprooted from an agriculturally based economy. In this sense his plays do cater, as Lope himself declared they ought in his *Arte nuevo de hacer comedias*, to the desires of the audience.[6] They speak to the pain and anger of a displaced urban community no longer supported by the values the plays enshrine, allowing them to channel their resentment against the "bad guys" who represent book learning and the destruction of the popular culture.

In Lope's *Fuenteovejuna* the rustic simplicities of plain language, communal feelings, simple foods, loyalty to the king, and marital fidelity are set off against the decadence of the excessive schooling, hedonism, and individualism of the noblemen of town and court. Lope's plays tend to associate loyalty to the king and marital fidelity with characters of old-Christian origin and peasant stock, while the villains are from the nobility. The nobles flaunt their education and power, threatening in the process to destroy not only the community, but the country as a whole.

In the theater of Calderón—a theater no less conservative than Lope's but aimed now not so much at the newly urbanized peasantry as at the nobility for whom court theaters were built during the reign of Philip IV (1621–65)—the easy distribution along class lines of good and evil characters so prevalent in the plays of Lope is no longer possible. While honor to king and father and marital fidelity remain central to the value system propagated in Calderón, the challenges to the institutions of patriarchy have moved in-house. Since both the upholder and the devaluer of the vaunted social norms can be found within the same social class, indeed, within the same family, class issues no longer claim center stage in the plays. What does persist, however, is the sense of danger facing the community from that which lies outside of it. The community—whether rural or urban, peasant or noble—is one held together by patriarchal values. It is menaced—whether by noblemen or by servants, rebels, and women—by those characters who have no place within its structure.[7]

What Calderón shows so strikingly—as we shall see in the particular case of *La vida es sueño*—is that it doesn't matter whether the outsider is a villain or a victim. His or her very presence as an entity unnamed or unaccounted for by the system requires that he or she be eliminated. The drama in the hands of Calderón is clearly the consummate instrument of literacy, the genre most thoroughly implicated in the written word's pretense to substance, and therefore the genre most deeply committed to preserving its fictions of presence and authority against the ever-present undertow of absence and meaninglessness.

When, as with *Lazarillo de Tormes* and *Don Quixote* before Calderón's time, and with Derrida in our own, the fact of the abandoning father and the wayside (and wayward) mother is directly confronted, the result is a text in which meaning and determinacy are radically called into question, in which all notions of hierarchy—conceptual as well as social—are relativized. In Calderón, writing for an entrenched and embattled nobility in a medium by its very nature oriented toward the tastes and values of the dominant social group, the drama revolves around the problem of upholding patriarchal structures in the face of a consistently debased image of father, king, and husband.[8]

Calderón's characters struggle, not surprisingly, for definition—to recover for themselves, out of the ever-impending threat of erasure, a solid sense of place and of meaning. Psychologically or otherwise, the issue in play after play revolves around a father who has abandoned his son, a husband who kills his wife, or a nobleman who abuses his privilege. And the point will be, in play after play, that however unjust their actions are, the figures who embody the patriarchy—father, husband, potentate—must prevail. Their presence is the determinant of order and context, and it falls inevitably on the characters who remain outside that order either to find a place within it, or to accept their death or expulsion.

To fail to see that it doesn't really matter whether the rejected characters are reconciled with the social order or not is to misread these plays. The given, in every case, is that the individual is subordinate to the structure.[9] And so we find, in Calderón, a forced reinstallation of the "nuclear family" that the written culture has in fact destroyed. The new identity—mother/culture, father/authority—is one now removed from the passions, the flesh, and the oral culture that literacy has supplanted. The new matrix in which the word finds meaning is the social structure, a structure removed from the hurly-burly of desire, and independent of reference to the material world. And the new authority is the word of the king. The king's consort is no fleshly, birth-giving, passion-centered woman, but the social order, fixed, unchanging. The character who would join this new family cannot attain a place within it simply by being of woman born. He must be born again into it, and born again by rejecting the ties of flesh and passion which threaten the order.

La vida es sueño (1635) is one of Calderón's best-known, and yet most puzzling plays. Successive generations have wondered over its many seeming anomalies, asking, for example, how it is that Calderón's perfect prince—the figure Segismundo comes to embody at the end of the play—could incarcerate the very soldier who supported his right to the throne.[10] Critics also continue to wrestle with the question of Rosaura's role in the play. Although her struggle for identity parallels that of Segismundo, and although her presence in his life has a powerful catalytic effect, the perfect prince that Segismundo becomes is called upon to renounce his love for her.[11] Critical readings of the play also tend to grapple with the confused process of transformation undergone by Segismundo: why is it particularly logical to conclude, because "life is a dream," that one must therefore strive to "obrar bien," to "do good works"? The question becomes even more vexing when we realize that Segismundo must finally know that he was tricked—that the experience in the palace that he was told was only a dream was not in fact a dream at all.[12]

The complications that have inhibited understanding of *La vida es sueño* dissolve when we recognize at the outset that the play is dealing not so much with a crisis in the life of Segismundo as with the survival of the social structure when that which guarantees it—the figure of the king—loses its pretense to invulnerability. *La vida es sueño* focuses on the question of succession in a system built on the illusion of permanence. It throws into conflict, in other words, the mutually exclusive notions of synchrony and diachrony, and with it, the equally incompatible claims of nature and culture. It asks, as it probes the difficulties of replacing the father with the son, the more general question of how any system can incorporate within it those terms that challenge its all-sufficiency.

The play locates itself at the fulcrum point where failed words and ineffective images require the ingestion of new information in order to restore their lost grounding in experience. At that fulcrum point are centered the very issues the system is otherwise occupied in keeping veiled: the issues of birth and death, of procreation and succession. These are the places of horror and fascination at which the system, otherwise self-enclosed, self-sufficient, and nonreferential—is forced to ingest elements foreign to itself, to expose itself to the truth of its alienation and meaninglessness.

By drawing attention to the moment when the failures in the system are beginning to show, Calderón invites his audience to experience the vertigo of a world without system, only to end by shutting the doors tight once again, returning us once again to the safety of enclosure. The king, Basilio, is old as the play begins. He is yielding, as his nephew Astolfo says, "to time's familiar disdain" ("al común desdén del

tiempo," 1.5.534–35).[13] Since he is widowed and apparently without
a natural heir, the pretenders to the throne have materialized in the
form of his niece Estrella and his nephew Astolfo—offspring of his two
younger sisters. The two aspirants to the throne plan, in Act 1, a political marriage so as peacefully to succeed their uncle as rulers of Poland.

What the audience already knows and the aspiring cousins are soon
to find out, however, is that the peaceful succession they imagine is
threatened on two counts. Out in the fierce countryside, in that no-
man's-land where outsiders arrive within the borders of the established order—here represented by Poland—we have already encoun-
tered, beastly and raving, the king's dark secret. He has in fact had a
son, and therefore, by rights, there exists a legal heir to the throne.
That son, however, was born in most inauspicious circumstances, as
the king finally confesses to his niece and nephew toward the end of
Act 1. Out of fear of his infant son's destructive potential, he tells
them, he decided to announce that the child had died, and to have him
guarded in a tower in the wild terrain near the border.

What could easily be missed in Basilio's impassioned account of the
many signs the heavens gave of Segismundo's violent nature is that
birth itself introduces chaos into the serene order that he has established. To die and to be born, Basilio points out, are similar ("el nacer
y morir son parecidos," 1.6.666–67). The theme is echoed by Segismundo, who has already cried out that man's greatest sin is to be born
("pues el delito meyor del hombre es haber nacido," 1.2.111–12), and
is a leitmotif in the theater of Calderón. One's salvation consists in dying to the flesh of that original birth. Basilio's manner of establishing
such a salvation is to retreat from the world. His success as a king is not
unrelated to his image as a man "more given to study than to women"
("más inclinado a los estudios que dado a mujeres," 1.5.535–37), a
"Wise Thales" who rules "against time and oblivion" ("contra el
tiempo y olvido," 1.6.579,607). Anyone who aspires to a place within
this kingdom will also be expected to sever his connection with woman, desire, the instincts, the flesh.

The denial of the flesh, of course, is provisional, and ultimately
time-bound. The king does age, the rejected son does grow up to make
his blood claim, the passions do insist. It is simply that the preservers
of the order must deny as long as possible these intrusions. Basilio, as

it turns out, is only one of a foursome of male characters all of whom will be called upon, in the name of the system, to refuse the flesh. All will do so as a matter of course, and all will be honored for their actions.

The opening scenes of Act 1 provide the spectacle of not one, but two characters living in no-man's-land. Both have been rejected by their fathers, and both struggle for self-definition in a labyrinthine world which offers no lexicon for their predicament. Besides Segismundo, whose speech is filled with oxymorons which declare their incapacity to provide him definition (he calls himself a "living skeleton" ["esqueleto vivo"] and an "a living dead man" ["animado muerto"] (1.2.201,202), we meet Rosaura, a woman dressed as a man, a Muscovite just entering Poland, a stranger, like Segismundo, without country or father.[14]

Rosaura's triple onus is to be from Moscow when the center of rule is Poland, to be illegitimate when paternal recognition establishes identity, and to be nonvirginal and unmarried, when being married requires virginity as a precondition. Only in the "manly" act of coming to Poland can she reclaim the identity the conditions of her birth have denied her. Her effort throughout the play will be to reclaim the recognition that both father and lover have heretofore refused her and to lose, thereby, her indeterminacy.

Rosaura, on threat of death for having inadvertently discovered Segismundo, tells her story to Clotaldo, the king's trusted tutor who has been given the task of guarding Segismundo and keeping secret his identity. Clotaldo quickly realizes, without so confessing, that the figure before him is his own child, and is horrified further to learn that she comes to Poland not so much to seek him out as to regain the honor she lost by becoming the lover of none other than the king's nephew and pretender to the throne, Astolfo.

By the end of Act 1 the story of courtly treachery has been fully exposed: Basilio, his wife Clorilene having died in childbirth, has rejected his son, banishing him to the life of a beast in the mountains at the kingdom's border; Clotaldo, having seduced Violante, the Muscovite mother of Rosaura, has abandoned both woman and child to find power in Poland; and Astolfo, having seduced and abandoned Rosaura in Moscow, has also come to Poland, hoping to become king by marrying his cousin Estrella. All of the men, having experienced the attractions of the flesh, have left women and children out of their lives in favor of a place of rule at court.[15]

Act 1 divides the two worlds represented in the play into two equal parts: on the one hand, in scenes 1 through 4, the violent countryside, inhabited by monstrous creatures, neither male nor female, neither beast nor man, neither living nor dead; on the other, in scenes 5 through 8, the court—serene, urbane, bloodless, peopled with characters fully identified with their position and role. The first scenes reveal the lies on which the social order that dominates the last scenes in the act depends.

In Act 2, the two opposing worlds that are so radically separated in Act 1 are brought together. Rosaura comes to court, now in woman's dress, under the name of Astrea. Segismundo, in a trial prepared by his father to test the stars ("I want to find out if the heavens, though it is not possible that they lie . . . might temper or lessen their decree"; "Quiero examinar si el cielo que no es posible que mienta . . . o se mitiga o se templa," 2.1.1102–03, 1106) also comes to court. The new amalgam of court and country proves disastrous. Segismundo, infuriated by the realization of his father's rejection, plays havoc with the conventions of court, killing a servant, attempting rape, and seeking revenge on Clotaldo and Basilio. Rosaura at court proves only slightly less embarrassing to the powers that be. She threatens to expose Astolfo's infidelity, thus ruining his chances to marry Estrella, and also puts at risk her father's honor, since if he were to acknowledge her as his daughter he would be obliged to kill Astolfo.

Only in Act 3, when the rejected figures return to their place of indefinition—Segismundo to his skins and imprisonment, Rosaura to her masculine attire—can the miracle of resolution take place. It takes place not by violent overthrow, however, though by now, word of Segismundo's existence having spread, the kingdom is divided and civil war threatens. The resolution takes place through the transformation of Segismundo. Deciding that there is no way to distinguish the lived experience of his life of imprisonment from the supposedly dreamed experience of life at court, he realizes that the choice of how to live is finally his. In a crucial confrontation between duty and desire—established when Rosaura, who has gotten nowhere with either Astolfo or Clotaldo, comes to the country to beg his support—Segismundo lays aside his own desire for Rosaura and opts instead to help her win back her rightful husband Astolfo. Segismundo choses the side of honor over that of passion because he associates the former with "the eternal" ("lo eterno," 3.10.2982), while the latter is "a beautiful flame that is turned to ash by any passing wind" ("llama hermosa que la convierte en cenizas cualquier viento que sopla," 3.10.2979–81). Segismundo, marshaling all of his willpower, goes against his passionate nature, resisting Rosaura's attractiveness, forgiving Clotaldo and Basilio, and, in the last scene, calling upon Astolfo to marry and Clotaldo to recognize Rosaura. In the end, honor is restored, and the successor to Basilio has peacefully ascended to the throne. The kingdom is intact.

By acting as he has acted, Segismundo completes the portrait of ruling male figures in the play, refusing, like Astolfo, Basilio, and Clotaldo, the seductions of feminine beauty. Segismundo wins his right to the throne, in fact, on that basis, for it was desire for Rosaura that colored all his actions up until 3.10, and refusal of that desire that made his decision of clemency toward Clotaldo and Basilio possible.

The crisis of succession is resolved in a relatively orderly fashion. It is ultimately orderly, however difficult the transition, because it preserves difference and hierarchy. No two people can ever occupy the same position at the same time within the system. Sexual encounter, on the other hand, represents a radical threat to difference and hierarchy and thus can never find a place within the social order. Segismundo's glorious resolution to the problem of succession is rarely understood to be intimately linked with, dependent on, in fact, the negation of sexual union. Procreation must always take place outside the bounds of the structure.

Segismundo's renunciation of desire for Rosaura affirms the very essence of the world Calderón depicts in *La vida es sueño*. Rosaura, as inspirer, as bringer of life, as a signifier of passion, is associated with the maternal world—with the emotions, the unconscious, the mother tongue, the oral culture—which must be kept out of a world whose order is defined by the law of the word of the father. The issues of the play are only finally resolved when each father confers identity on the offspring he has engendered. In so doing, he confers life, an identity, upon a being otherwise lost in the labyrinth. The fathers do not, however, reintegrate the mothers. Clorilene and Violante, the mothers of Segismundo and Rosaura, have no place in the final resolution.

What Calderón makes clear is that the ultimate scapegoat is not the male rival but the woman. Until Segismundo mandated it in the last lines of the last scene in Act 3, neither Astolfo nor Clotaldo was willing to accept responsibility for Rosaura. Both feared entanglement with the other in the form of violent confrontation if either accepted her in her "dishonored" state, and preferred instead to sacrifice her.[16] Woman comes into the structure only when her place is one agreed upon by all the men involved, and when that place fits into the already established order. Her presence as wife, therefore, is acceptable, but her presence as lover or mother triggers passions and emotions that destabilize the order. Thus the deep love that Segismundo has felt for Rosaura in all three acts of the play must be sacrificed if he is to take an exemplary place in his culture.

As René Girard has pointed out in numerous places, culture requires for its stability the rigorous maintenance of hierarchy and difference.[17] Its task is to expel ritually the threats to difference that simultaneity and identity present, and therefore, to expel that which suggests passion and desire. The expression of horror that simultaneity and identity evoke is represented in Calderón in the frequent elision in his works of sexual desire and incest.[18] Fear of history, of time, is but an aspect of an all-pervasive fear, throughout Calderón's works, of generativity, of breaking out of self-enclosed systems, of merging with something other.

The overcoming of the passions for which Segismundo is regularly applauded is intimately linked with the wife murders critics have scrambled to justify or explain in Calderón's honor plays. It all has to do with that heroic effort of intellect, alluded to at the beginning of this paper, to master the senses and the emotions, or, if not to master them, at least to keep them at bay. When the intellect is not in charge, in this view, chaos reigns. Basilio's description of Segismundo's birth perfectly captures the fear that the presence of birth and death inspire. On the day Segismundo was born, he says, "the two celestial lights entered into battle" ("los dos faroles divinos a luz entera luchaban," 1.6), and

The heavens darkened,	Los cielos se oscurecieron,
the buildings shook,	temblaron los edificios,
the clouds rained stones,	llovieron piedras las nubes,
the rivers ran blood.	corrieron sangre los ríos.

(1.6.696–99)

The constant linking of birth with death in the play, and of both with sin reveals a world in which terror is the psychic dominant. Anything, rather than open up again that fearful, bloody reminder of our contingency. Better the study of the stars, the refusal of the passions, the books, the tower.

We can now see, from the other side, the new linking of marriage and succession. Succession is simply the temporal expression of the marriage. It is the suppression of union in favor of conjunction. Succession is stalled marriage, the recognition of the need for the other, but the postponement of it out of fear. Succession grants a space of time during which one experiences peace, stability. It then requires, in payment, a sudden withdrawal of all that is peaceful, a fall into violence and confusion, which will then be followed, once again, by peace and stability. If we apply that model not only to the succession of kings, but to all moments of exchange, we see that what Calderón addresses in *La vida es sueño* is also the difficulty of allowing cultural and linguistic systems to acknowledge their connection to any reality outside themselves. Through the metaphors of violence, passion, and chaos Calderón reveals the degree to which the written culture has separated itself from the oral culture—the world of the mother—from which it arose. In place of the rejecting father it creates a spectral version of paternity and authority whose fallibility is only exposed at moments of crisis.

The problem confronted in *La vida es sueño* of opening the reigning order to change—of naming a new king and establishing the marriage partners for the next generation—comes ultimately to be a problem not only of succession and procreation but of referentiality, and, more specifically, a problem of acknowledging the otherwise suppressed existence of the other—the mother, the child, the countryside, life, death, desire, and the unconscious. The movement that takes place in Western Europe in the Renaissance from a primarily oral to a primarily literate culture provokes a whole series of rifts in consciousness, rifts reflected in the relation between word and thing, between author and audience, and—metaphorically at least—between parent and child. Both *Lazarillo de Tormes* and *Don Quixote* expose the emptiness, madness, and lawlessness that such rifts foster, revealing, at the same time, a nostalgia for the oral culture that has been left behind.

By the time Calderón writes *La vida es sueño* the print culture has become so entrenched in the consciousness of the elite that the mother and the unconscious are perceived no longer as objects of longing, but of threat and fear. Confronted with the seemingly uncontrollable realities of the world of life and blood and passion, the typical Calderonian hero recoils in fear and loathing. His task, if he is to become part of the "happy ending" that is the return of a threatened kingdom to order, is to abandon his investment in desire and the mother, and cling to the foster parent of the "maternal culture" whose father presides, like Basilio in his tower, over the system of differences which will temporarily house him.

In the world Calderón creates, the world of the immured written culture, the father has already abandoned the child, and the mother is already debased. That is the starting point, as it is in the life of Segismundo. Given that situation of orphanhood, the hero has only two choices: to give himself up to the situation Derrida described as the condition of the written word, to wander, without responsibility or consciousness, or to accept the temporary shelter of the foster home, as Greene has suggested that words do. When Segismundo takes up his place at the end as his father's successor, he does so knowing that the place he has won is temporary: that in the tower a rebel soldier rages, that in the court Rosaura continues to attract with a desire that cannot be permitted to find expression, that despite all astrological and mathematical formulas, time will finally have its way. But for the moment, there is meaning.

Notes

[1]Greene's effort to reserve a place for meaning in the light of Derrida's discussions on the nature of language occupies the bulk of his chapter 1. The quote from Derrida comes from "Signature Event Context," and is cited in Greene's book on 11. The citation appears in the English translation on 181.

[2]The bibliography on the subject has become rich in the last decade. Among the most influential American studies are Dinnerstein, Rich, Miller, and Chodorow.

[3]The metaphor also validates the presupposition of modern psychology from Freud through Lacan that culture, and, more basically, the resolution of the child's frustrated

desire to remain one with the mother, is structured around the assimilation of the word of the father.

[4]Havelock makes clear the intimate connection between a sense of the self as autonomous and the development of a written culture, studying the emergence of that process in Greek culture from Homer to Plato. In the *Republic* Plato exhorts a rejection of poetry as a model for learning because of its association with the identifactory processes through which knowledge is transmitted in an oral culture. As Havelock puts it, "The doctrine of the autonomous psyche is the counterpart of the rejection of the oral culture" (200). The process was reactivated on a mass scale in the Renaissance when the invention of the printing press created the conditions for the education of young boys on a scale never before known. For more on this see Walter J. Ong, "Latin Language Study as a Renaissance Puberty Rite," in *Rhetoric, Romance and Technology,* and "Transformations of the Word and Alienation" in *Interfaces of the Word.*

[5]See Ong's "Media Transformation: The Talked Book," in *Interfaces of the Word,* and also "From Epithet to Logic: Miltonic Epic and the Closure of Existence" in the same volume. In the latter article he says " . . . the epic, even when written, remains in some way essentially oral and . . . the drama, despite its oral presentation, is essentially a written genre, the genre first (from Greek antiquity) completely controlled by writing. . . . A dramatic hero is not entirely commensurate with an epic hero. . . . The drama, more perhaps than other genres, abetted the development of chirographic noetic structures and states of consciousness" (212 n. 32).

[6]Lope defends his practice of giving the audience what it wants in his long poem *Arte nuevo de hacer comedias en este tiempo* (1609).

[7]No one better than Edwin Honig has seen how women and nonaristocratic characters stand in Calderón's plays as figures of threat: "In the autocratic society of Calderón's plays, every family seems to be a miniature Spain seeking to preserve itself against the real or imagined, but always chronic, invasions of lawless forces from outside" (61).

[8]A. A. Parker, in "Santos y bandoleros en el teatro espãnol del siglo de oro," notes how central to Calderón's dramaturgy is the problem of the father as flawed patriarch: "He [Calderón] saw that the question of paternal authority had complicated shades of meaning, and in his theater the moral upheaval that the abuse of that authority could cause a son came to be a fundamental problem that greatly preoccupied him" (402–03; translation mine). See also Parker's "The Father-Son Conflict in the Drama of Calderón."

[9]This subordination of individual to society is a characteristic of Calderonian theater that has allowed critics to insist on the nontragic essence of the theater of the Christian baroque that Calderón so well represents. A. A. Parker has pointed out in "Towards a Definition of Calderonian Tragedy" that the "self-assertive construction of a private world of one's own is, for Calderón, the root of moral evil" (223). Henry W. Sullivan and Ellie Ragland-Sullivan update the notion of Christian tragedy, giving it a Lacanian twist, but maintaining, essentially like Parker, that success—a happy ending—is one in which the individual submits to the "law of the name-of-the-father."

[10]The debate on the justification of imprisoning the rebel solider has engaged the passions of a great many critics. Some of the best-known articles on the subject are: Parker, "Calderón's Rebel Soldier and Poetic Justice"; May; Halkhoree; Connolly; and Heiple. See also Cesáreo Bandera.

[11]See, for example, Sloman, Whitby, Wilson, and de Armas.

[12]Lipmann takes up insightfully the relationship between epistemological and moral problems at the end of the play. Among other commentators who have discussed the relationship between the intuition that life is a dream and Segismundo's conversion are Sloman, Pring-Mill, and Hesse.

[13]All citations will give act and scene and line number. The translations into English are my own.

[14]Echevarría also addresses, through the image of the monster, the question of expression as experienced through Calderón's plays. He says: "'The monstrosity of differing species,' then, turns out to be two things: on the one hand a logical or discursive impossibility, since it deals with simultaneously contradictory predicates; on the other, an impossible vision, ambiguous, difficult to interpret, made up of appearances in conflict. . . . the essence of the monstrosity of differing species is its changing nature, which cannot be captured in language" (translation mine).

[15]The generality of this decision in Calderón's plays is pointed out by Honig when he says, "there is an underlying assumption [in Calderonian drama] that women, like poets, madmen, and devils, are as fascinating as they are dangerous and disruptive. . . . Women subsist on the margins of the serious life; they have nothing to do with the business of living in a world charged with purpose, patrimony, and passionate missions" (22).

[16]Borinsky points out the timelessness of the male bonding system, built on the elimination of an otherwise conflict-producing woman, by showing its presence in Calderón's *A secreto agravio secreta venganza*, and Borges's short story, "La intrusa."

[17]The question is most vigorously probed in *Violence and the Sacred*, though references to issues of difference and hierarchy recur throughout Girard's work. For other clear statements regarding "degree," or difference, see "Myth and Ritual" and "The Plague."

[18]The topic is taken up, with special reference to *La vida es sueño*, in Gisele Feal and Carlos Feal-Deibe's "Calderón's *Life Is a Dream*: From Psychology to Myth." The incest motif is more overt, however, in other plays by Calderón, most notably *La hija del aire, Los cabellos de Absolón,* and *La devoción de la cruz*. Commenting on the last play Honig says, "In effect the Genesis story demonstrates an archetypal incest situation inherent in man's disobedience, his fall from God's grace, and his knowledge of good and evil. Taken as a paradigm for man's earthly condition, the sexual crime called original sin derives from a transgression against divine command, a transgression that brings with it the knowledge of guilt."

Works Cited

BANDERA, CESÁREO. *Mimesis conflictiva*. Madrid: Gredos, 1975. 253–60.

BORINSKY, ALICIA. "Benefits of Anachronism: A Disorder in Calderón Papers." *The Rhetoric of Feminist Writing*. Ed. Diana Wilson. *Denver Quarterly* 18 (1984): 84–93.

CHODOROW, NANCY. *The Reproduction of Mothering: Psychoanalysis and the Sociology of Gender*. Berkeley: U of California P, 1979.

CONNOLLY, EILEEN M. "Further Testimony on the Rebel Soldier Case." *BCom* 24 (1972): 11–15.

DE ARMAS, FREDERICK. "The Return of Astraea." *Calderón de la Barca At the Tercentenary: Comparative Views*. Lubbock: Texas Tech P, 1982. 135–59.

DERRIDA, JACQUES, "Signature Event Context." *Glyph I*. Baltimore and London: Johns Hopkins UP, 1977. 172–97.

DINNERSTEIN, DOROTHY. *The Mermaid and the Minotaur: Sexual Arrangements and Human Malaise*. New York: Harper, 1976.

ECHEVARRÍA, ROBERTO GONZÁLEZ. "El 'monstruo de una especie y otra'." *Calderón: Códigos, monstruos, Icones*. Centre d'Etudes et Recherches Sociocritiques, 1982. 27–58.

FEAL, GISÈLE, and CARLOS FEAL-DEIBE. "Calderon's *Life Is a Dream*: From Psychology to Myth." *Hartford Studies in Literature* 6 (1974): 1–28.

GIRARD, RENÉ. "Myth and Ritual in Shakespeare." *Textual Strategies: Perspectives in Post-Structuralist Criticism*. Ed. Josué V. Harari. Ithaca: Cornell UP, 1979.

_____. "The Plague in Literature and Myth." *To Double Business Bound*. Baltimore: Johns Hopkins UP, 1978.

_____. *Violence and the Sacred*. Trans. Patrick Gregory. Baltimore: Johns Hopkins UP, 1972.

GREENE, THOMAS. *The Light in Troy: Imitation and Discovery in Renaissance Poetry*. New Haven and London: Yale UP, 1982.

HALKHOREE, P. "A Note on the Ending of Calderón's *La vida es sueño*." *BCOM* 24 (1972): 8–11.

HAVELOCK, ERIC A. *Preface to Plato*. Cambridge: Harvard UP, 1963.

HEIPLE, DANIEL L. "The Tradition Behind the Punishment of the Rebel Soldier in *La vida es sueño*." *BHS* 50 (1973): 1–17.

HESSE, EVERETT. "El motivo del sueño en *La vida es sueño*." *Segismundo* 3 (1967): 55–67.

HONIG, EDWIN. *Calderón and the Seizures of Honor*. Cambridge: Harvard UP, 1972.

LIPMANN, STEPHEN. "Segismundo's Fear at the End of *La Vida es sueño*." *MLN* 97 (1982): 380–90.

MAY, T. E. "Segismundo y el soldado rebelde." *Hacia Calderon*. Ed. H. Flasche. Berlin: Walter de Gruyter, 1970. 71–75.

MILLER, JEAN BAKER. *Toward a New Psychology of Women*. Boston: Beacon, 1976.

ONG, WALTER J. *Interfaces of the Word*. Ithaca and London: Cornell UP, 1977.

———. *Rhetoric, Romance and Technology*. Ithaca and London: Cornell UP, 1971.

PARKER, A. A. "Calderón's Rebel Soldier and Poetic Justice." *BHS* 46 (1969): 120–27.

———. "The Father-Son Conflict in the Drama of Calderón." *Forum for Modern Language Studies* 2 (1966): 99–113.

———. "Santos y bandoleros en el teatro español del siglo de oro." *Arbor* 43–44 (1949): 395–416.

———. "Towards a Definition of Calderonian Tragedy." *BHS* 39 (1962): 222–37.

PRING-MILL, R.D.F. "La victoria del hado en *La vida es sueño*." *Hacia Calderón*. Ed. H. Flasche. Berlin: Walter de Gruyter, 1970. 53–70.

RICH, ADRIENNE. *Of Woman Born: Motherhood as Experience and Institution*. New York: Harper, 1976.

SLOMAN, A. E. "The Structure of Calderón's *La vida es sueño*." *MLR* 48 (1953): 293–300.

SULLIVAN, HENRY W., and ELLIE RAGLAND-SULLIVAN. "*Las tres justicias en una* of Calderón and the Question of Christian Catharsis." *Critical Perspectives on Calderon de la Barca*. Eds. José A. Madrigal, David Gitlitz, et al. Lincoln, NE: Society for Spanish and Spanish-American Studies, 1981. 119–190.

VEGA CARPIO, LOPE FÉLIX DE. "Arte nuevo de hacer comedias en este tiempo." 1609. *Dramatic Theory in Spain*. Ed. H. J. Chaytor. Cambridge: Clarendon, 1925, 14–29.

WHITBY, WILLIAM M. "Rosaura's Role in the Structure of *La vida es sueño*." *HR* 27 (1960): 16–27.

WILSON, E. M. "On *La vida es sueño*." *Critical Essays on the Theater of Calderón*. Ed. Bruce W. Wardropper. New York: New York UP, 1965.

Temporality, Anachronism, and Presence in Shakespeare's English Histories

PHYLLIS RACKIN

THE DOUGLAS, says Prince Hal, is reputed to be such a good shot that he can kill a flying sparrow with his pistol (2.4.344–45). The Variorum edition of *1 Henry IV* reminds us that pistols were not yet invented in the days of Henry IV; but without such a footnote, modern readers are likely to miss the anachronism. And even if we do notice it, we have all been instructed that neither Shakespeare nor his original audience was troubled by such inconsistencies.

Critical thinking about Shakespeare's use of temporality has not changed very much in the two hundred years since Dr. Johnson wrote his own footnote on the Douglas's pistol—"Shakespeare never has any care to preserve the manners of the time" (Variorum 157n)—and his famous rebuttal of the neoclassical critics who thought Shakespeare's Romans not sufficiently Roman and his kings not sufficiently royal: "His story requires Romans or kings, but he thinks only on men." For us, as for Johnson, Shakespeare is still the great poet of "general nature" (Preface 331). With his eye on the eternal verities, Shakespeare could hardly be expected to anticipate the cavils of pedants that the conspirators in *Julius Caesar* wear anachronistic hats and Antony's

Cleopatra lived too soon to play at billiards and the Douglas kills sparrows with a not-yet-invented firearm.

There is no doubt that many of Shakespeare's anachronisms went unnoticed by most members of his original audience, who were not likely to be disturbed when they saw Posthumus wave a glove in the first-century England of Cymbeline any more than they worried about the location of the seacoast in Bohemia.[1] Shakespeare was no more meticulous about the dates of historical events than he was about the literal details of geography. Still, place is never treated as insignificant in Shakespeare's plays. It is generally understood that Shakespeare was careless about geography, but only because he had better things to do with his settings than plot their locations on a map, and twentieth-century criticism has become highly sophisticated in its treatment of Shakespearean settings.

The elaborate archaeological reconstructions and realistic local color of nineteenth-century productions have given way to the recognition that the action of a Shakespearean scene, designed to be performed on a bare stage, is often set in a kind of neutral space. We know that unless the action localizes the scene or one of the characters says something like, "Well, this is the forest of Arden," there is no reason to suppose that the stage represents any particular place (Styan 44–46). And we know too that the very lack of a generally assumed location means that when Shakespeare does localize a scene, the location is likely to be significant, not simply as a place where a particular event occurs, but as a milieu which defines and participates in the dramatic action. Thus, Rome and Egypt in *Antony and Cleopatra* are not simply states but also states of mind, and the green and gray worlds of Shakespearean comedy echo with symbolic resonance. Different worlds call forth different kinds of action; and similar actions played out in different worlds have strikingly different consequences and evoke radically different responses from an audience.

I would like to suggest that Shakespeare's use of time can be understood in much the same way that we have learned to understand his use of space—that temporality, anachronism, and presence all represent deliberate, significant choices which color the meaning of a dramatic action and define the nature of the relationship established between the events depicted on stage and the audience watching them in a theater. Shakespeare uses time in a variety of ways, even within the course of a single play. Sometimes he localizes the action in a particular historical period—the fourteenth century of Richard II, for instance, or the ancient Rome of Julius Caesar, or the still more ancient Rome of Coriolanus. At other times, he deliberately dislocates the action, using anachronisms like the clock that strikes in *Julius Caesar*[2] to allow characters from different ages and cultures to meet as Bottom and Flute and Snout, sixteenth-century English workmen, can mingle on a midsummer night in the enchanted woods outside Athens with a legendary Greek hero like Theseus and imaginary Greek characters like Demetrius, Hermia, Lysander, and Helena. In short, I would like to argue that a crucial Shakespearean strategy is the manipulation of the temporal relationship between past events and present audience and that Shakespeare uses this strategy in his history plays to dramatize the distance and the intersection between past and present, eternity and time, and to ponder the problematic nature of history itself.

For Shakespeare's contemporaries, the nature of history was especially problematic because old and new methods of historiography were competing for ascendancy. In England, the sixteenth century saw the invention, not only of the English history play, but of history itself.[3] There were no chairs of history at the English universities until the seventeenth century (Levy 49–50; Ferguson 30), and at the beginning of the sixteenth century English writers made no clear distinction between history and poetry, either of which could be written in prose or verse and both of which freely mingled fact and legend, event and interpretation, and endowed characters from the past with the customs and manners of the present.[4] By the seventeenth century, all this had changed: history had become an autonomous discipline with its own purposes and methods, clearly distinct from myth and literature (Ferguson 36–38). Two great innovations made these distinctions possible, both originating in Italy and both affecting English historiography during the second half of the sixteenth century. The first was the gradual separation of history from theology: explanations of events in terms of their first cause in Divine Providence were giving way to Machiavellian analysis of second causes—the effects of political situations and the impact of human will and capabilities. The new "politic historians" still made reference to the will of God as the first cause behind historical change, but they described historical causation primarily in terms of "second causes," that is, of human actions and their consequences; and they evaluated actions more in terms of their expediency, less in terms of their morality (Levy 237–85).

The second great innovation in English Renaissance historiography, also introduced from Italy, was the development of the concept of anachronism. Typically, medieval writers of history display no sense of anachronism: for them, all history is present history; Theseus and Alexander the Great are knights; and the customs, clothing, and manners of the historians' own times are uncritically ascribed to other times and places. It was not until the Renaissance, with the new recognition that the past was genuinely different from the present, that historians questioned the authenticity of venerable records which had been accepted for centuries despite the fact that they used a vocabulary and referred to objects that were unknown at the time of their supposed origin.[5]

Both of these changes—the new interest in second causes and the new awareness of anachronism—led not only to an increased concern with the authenticity of historical records but also to an increased sense of the differences between poetry and history. By the end of the sixteenth century, English writers generally agreed that poetry and history had distinct purposes—history teaching political wisdom while poetry taught moral virtue—and distinct methods—historians obliged to report the past accurately and to follow the "true" and "natural" order of events as they had happened, while poets might alter and rearrange historical material for maximum impact upon their readers or audiences (Levy 242–44; Ferguson 28–37, 42–43).

Within this context, the use of anachronisms in poetry was much debated. Medieval and early Renaissance poets, like their contemporary historians, displayed no sense of anachronism, and many writers besides Shakespeare continued to use anachronisms right through the sixteenth century. Apropos of the Douglas's pistol, for instance, the Variorum *I Henry IV* notes that "Beaumont and Fletcher, in *The Humorous Lieutenant* [a play written around 1620] have equipped one of the immediate successors of Alexander the Great with a pistol" (157n). At the same time, there were many critics to deplore such practices. Torquato Tasso, for instance, writing in 1594, compared a poet who uses anachronisms to "a painter of little judgment who presents a figure of Cato or Cincinnatus clothed according to the fashions of the young men of Milan or Naples" or gives Hercules "a doublet and helmet as Giraldi did in his poem" (482–83). Writing even earlier than Tasso, in 1571, Castelvetro criticized Sophocles for reporting a chariot race at the Pythian games in his *Electra* because "history makes evident" that the race was not part of the games at the time represented in the play (356–57). And even those writers who defended the use of anachronisms, like the unfortunate Giraldi Cinthio, the object of Tasso's ridicule, defended them as deliberate choices, dictated by the differences between poetry and history, not as insignificant lapses, unlikely to be noticed by a poet's audience. In Cinthio's view, a poet is not simply permitted but *obliged* to use anachronisms because his purpose is different from a historian's. Poets, Cinthio says, do "not write of things as they were or are, but as they should be." Unlike historians, poets who write of ancient affairs introduce "things unlike those of ancient times and suitable to their own" in order to "harmonize them with their own customs and their own age" and satisfy "the men of that age in which they write, a thing not permitted to those who write histories" (270–71).[6]

Thus, Shakespeare's use of anachronisms in the history plays must be seen as a self-conscious choice, a deliberate use of a method that distinguished the poet from the historiographer and formed the subject of acrimonious debate. Moreover, it was a method that did not go unnoticed among some, at least, in Shakespeare's original audience. On the day before their unsuccessful uprising against Queen Elizabeth, followers of the Earl of Essex sponsored a performance of *Richard II,* apparently hoping that the play would incite its audience to join their rebellion. A tiny anachronism, not likely to attract attention in a modern theater, occurs in Act 2, scene 1, when one of the fourteenth-century conspirators against King Richard charges that the king has used benevolences to extort money from his subjects. Shakespeare may have known that Richard II never used the forced loans called benevolences; for Holinshed, his source for most of the history plays, states that benevolences were introduced by Edward IV, who reigned late in the following century, and the authorities in Elizabeth's England certainly knew that Richard II never used benevolences because this very

anachronism—present not only in Shakespeare's play but also in a se-
ditious *Life of Henry VIII* by Sir John Hayward—was cited at the trial
of Essex as evidence that "the times of Elizabeth rather than those of
Richard II were in question."[7]

Not every anachronism had such profound or dangerous implications; many of them, I am convinced, would have passed without
comment. Often, Shakespeare simply takes advantage of a customary
poetic license to rearrange events within the historical time frame of
his play, telescoping two or three battles into one decisive encounter,
altering the order in which events occurred, or manipulating the ages
of historical characters to make a dramatic point. Thus, in *Henry IV*
Hotspur is made the contemporary of Prince Hal so he can serve as a
foil to the heir apparent, and thus Henry VI's Queen Margaret is kept
alive in the England of Richard III to rail at the Yorkists and remind the
audience of the past crimes that make their present sufferings justified.

Anachronisms like these, involving alterations of the order of events
within a historical context, may or may not be noticed by an audience,
for all the events remain situated within history: they are still told, as it
were, in the past tense. On the other hand, anachronisms that disrupt
the historical context to create direct confrontations between past and
present are more radical in their effect. The very essence of history is
that it deals with the past, with events that have already taken place.
Therefore, any invocation of the present in a history play tends to create radical dislocations: it invades the time frame of the audience, and
its effect is no less striking than that of a character stepping off the
stage to invade the audience's space or addressing them directly to invade their psychological space.

This type of anachronism, when the characters in a history play
break out of history to confront an audience directly, often produces a
kind of alienation effect. Thus, when the conspirators in *Julius Caesar*
say, "How many ages hence / Shall this our lofty scene be acted over /
In states unborn and accents yet unknown! how many times shall Caesar bleed in sport" (3.1. 111–13), we are reminded of our situation in
the playhouse and the actors' status as actors representing an event
that took place long ago when even the language the actors now speak
was yet unknown. When Henry V foretells, before the battle of Agincourt, that "Crispin Crispian shall ne'er go by, / From this day to the

ending of the world, / But we in it shall be remembered" (4.3.57–59), the audience is reminded that what they are seeing on stage is the reenactment of a historical moment that passed many years ago and survives for them only in the form of oral tradition and historical records.

Allusions within the context of a history play to the existence of that record are double-edged. On the one hand, they tend to break the contact between past events and present audience, for they remind an audience of the vast gulf of time and awareness that separates them from the historical characters portrayed on stage. On the other hand, they create an illusion of presence: by invoking the future, the historical characters are invoking the audience's present, stepping out of their historical situations to meet the audience in a neutral zone where all time is eternally present. Like Christ speaking from the cross to an audience at a medieval mystery play, they engage the audience directly in events that are no longer seen as reenacted or represented but as present action.[8]

A major attraction that draws an audience to a history play is the desire for just such an experience of presence. As Thomas Nashe wrote in praise of the English history plays,

our forefathers valiant acts (that have line long buried in rustie brasse and worme-eaten bookes) are revived, and they themselves raised from the Grave of Oblivion . . . How would it have joyed brave *Talbot* (the terror of the French) to thinke that after he had lyne two hundred yeares in his Tombe, hee should triumphe againe on the Stage, and have his bones newe embalmed with the teares of ten thousand spectators . . . who . . . imagine they behold him fresh bleeding? (238–39)[9]

The audience, as Nashe reminds us, went to the play hoping to see those historical records brought to life and to make direct contact with the living reality that was celebrated but also obscured by the "worm-eaten" books of history.

Shakespeare provides his audience with that experience, but he also uses his history plays to ponder the problematic nature of historical truth. For what an audience learns when it watches Shakespeare's history plays is that the full truth about history was no more accessible to the fourteenth- and fifteenth-century characters portrayed on stage than it is to their sixteenth-century descendants laboring to discover the living truth that lay behind the historical records. What the sixteenth-century audience lacks is direct experience of the actions recorded in the history books; what the participants in those actions lacked was the teleological understanding that would not be available until those history books had been written and future generations could evaluate the historical actions in terms of the consequences they would have.

Dramatic irony is thus endemic to the history play. The characters have moments of prophetic inspiration, but the audience is always gifted with hindsight, knowing how the story will come out even as it watches the characters agonize over their choices or struggle to avert their destinies. When Henry V predicts that his victory at Agincourt will be celebrated every year on St. Crispin's day, the audience knows he is right; but when he predicts that he and the French princess will breed a soldier son who will "go to Constantinople and take the Turk by the beard" (5.2.208–09) the audience knows how terribly wrong he is. And the Chorus, the voice of recorded history in the play, breaks in at the end to underscore the irony of Henry's confident prediction by reminding the audience of what they already knew about Henry VI's disastrous reign.

But the irony also reaches out to implicate the audience. If the choral voice in *Henry V,* or the interior choral voice that the members of the audience brought to the theater (i.e., their own prior knowledge of the received version of the history Shakespeare's actors were depicting)—if that choral voice knows things the characters depicted on stage could never know, its own version of events is not allowed to rest unquestioned or unassailed. This conflict between the received history and the events depicted on stage is plainest in *Henry V,* where the anachronistic Chorus, which talks about Essex's sixteenth-century expedition to Ireland and recites the conventional sixteenth-century pieties about the legendary "mirror of all Christian kings," is repeatedly contradicted by the events depicted on stage.[10] At the beginning of Act 4, for instance, the Chorus tells us that we will see Henry's untroubled good cheer on the eve of the battle of Agincourt, but the Henry we actually see in that act has a 55-line soliloquy of painful complaint. The conflict in this play between what the Chorus tells us and what we see is so striking, in fact, that modern critics of the play are still debating which account the audience is meant to believe.[11] In the earlier history plays, the conflict is not projected in such overt terms, but it still underlies their dynamics; for the audience always enters the theater with a historical version in mind, and the play always works to question and qualify that account.

In fact, one way to describe the dynamics of Shakespeare's history plays is to say that the audience is confronted with the task of reconciling its experience in the theater with its prior understanding of the events depicted in the play. The theater can make the past present, but that very presence entails its own limitations, for once an audience becomes involved in the messy human ambiguities of the events, it is forced to question the comfortable platitudes to which those events had been reduced in the history books. On the other hand, Shakespeare never allows his audience to dismiss the received versions, for he, no less than they, is finally bound to come to terms with them. Thus, the audience is placed in the uncomfortable position of trying to reconcile two opposed versions of the historical events, each of which insists upon the limitations of the other.

As Herbert Lindenberger has pointed out, "The action of historical drama is more precisely a struggle for legitimacy than a struggle for power" (160). This struggle represented in the play finds its analogue in the struggle within the minds of members of the audience as they try to decide where to place their allegiance as they watch the play. Typically, Shakespeare arranges his action to subvert the allegiances prescribed by Tudor history, forcing his audience to struggle painfully with dissonances between the verdict of history and the rhetoric of the play and allowing them to reconcile the two versions only at the ends of his plays and only in a radically qualified fashion.[12] Thus, it is not simply or even primarily the differences in detail that the audience must seek to reconcile: it is the differences in interpretation which are produced by the shifting temporal perspective, by seeing a historical event both within its own temporal context as a record of human choices and actions and seeing it within a grand, providential scheme as a manifestation of the will of God.

This process can be seen at its simplest level in Shakespeare's treatment of Joan in *1 Henry VI*. Joan had received very different treatment from French and English historians, and Shakespeare's audience was undoubtedly prepared to accept the English claims. According to Edward Hall, Shakespeare's main source for the play, Joan was a "wytch" who told such "visions, traunses, and fables, full of blasphemy, supersticion and hypocrisy, that I marvell much that wise men did beleve her, and lerned clarkes would write suche phantasies" (148). In *1 Henry VI,* Shakespeare encourages a no-doubt skeptical audience to believe those fantasies, for he not only has characters report them but stages them before the audience's very eyes. Hall reports with indignant skepticism, "What should I reherse, how they saie, she knewe and called hym her kyng, whom she never saw before. What should I speake how she had by revelacion a swerde, to her appoynted in the churche of saincte Katheryn, of Fierboys in Torayne where she neuer had been" (148). Shakespeare, in contrast, validates the story of the sword by having Joan use it to defeat the Dauphin in single combat to prove her claim to divine inspiration. As for the story of Joan's recognizing the Dauphin, Shakespeare dramatizes the miracle as present action on stage, embellishing it and making Joan's task more difficult by having the Dauphin attempt to conceal his identity.

Shakespeare disorients his audience by presenting the French as well as the English version of Joan, mostly by conflicting report, and it is not until the end that he resolves their dilemma by showing Joan consorting with evil spirits, attempting to escape death by claiming she is pregnant, and generally vindicating all the worst charges that the English chroniclers and the English characters in the play have brought against her. Up until that point, the audience is left in confusion, desperately torn between a patriotic desire to believe the worst of Joan and the contradictory evidence of her courage and miraculous powers, not only recounted, but also presented on the stage. Nonetheless, in this play the process is relatively simple: the audience is placed in the role of a historian trying to make sense out of conflicting evidence and opposed interpretations of events, and at the end of the play, it is allowed to come to rest in the received English version.

A more complicated version of the same process can be seen in the later histories, especially in *Richard II,* written about five years later. The basic dialectical process is here complicated by elaborate manipulations of the audience's temporal relationship to the action depicted on stage. As the play opens, it is clearly a period piece, designed to thrill its sixteenth-century audience with a glimpse of a remote and exotic medieval world. The opening line of the play, "Old John of Gaunt, time-honored Lancaster," in addition to its obvious literal meaning as the king's address to his venerable uncle, also sets the medieval scene for Shakespeare's audience by its reference to the legendary John of Gaunt, Chaucer's patron, who was indeed "time-honored" by the sixteenth century. And the elaborate pageantry of the opening scene reinforces the effect of a period piece, a play where we will see what the Tudor historians reported as the last of the great medieval trials by battle and the deposition of the last of the medieval kings, "ruling by hereditary right, direct and undisputed, from the Conqueror" with "the full sanctity of medieval kingship."[13]

Richard's reign, however, was interesting to the Elizabethans not only for its quaint pastness but also for its causal and analogical connections to their own present. The Tudor myth rationalized the sufferings of the Wars of the Roses as punishment for the deposition of Richard II, being God's vengeance upon the land that had deposed God's anointed king, and Elizabethan analogies between Richard II and Elizabeth I served as disquieting reminders that the tragic process might yet be reenacted on the stage of history as well as Shakespeare's theater.[14]

Tudor historians described Richard's faults and errors as a ruler, but although Bolingbroke's usurpation of Richard's throne was explained as a result of Bolingbroke's legitimate grievances and Richard's own faults, it was also interpreted in terms of first causes as a transgression against God for which the entire country would have to suffer until it was finally expiated in blood and Henry VII and Elizabeth of York, Queen Elizabeth's grandparents, could restore legitimacy to the throne. This teleological reading of history established a direct line of providential purpose between the long-ago-deposed Plantagenet king and the reigning Tudor queen. There were analogical connections as well. As I have argued elsewhere, Queen Elizabeth's often-quoted comment, "I am Richard II, know ye not that?"; the sponsorship by Essex's followers of a performance of an old play about Richard II (probably Shakespeare's) on the afternoon before their rebellion; and the suppression of the deposition scene in Shakespeare's play during the queen's lifetime all indicate that for Shakespeare's audience the play was not simply an exercise in historical re-creation or an occasion for nostalgia.[15]

Thus history in *Richard II* is presented to the audience from two opposed temporal perspectives—as a quaint, static representation, told in the past tense, of actions already completed and reduced to the stasis of historical tableaux, and as a living present process that reaches out to involve and implicate the audience in the theater. At the beginning of the play, the audience is introduced to a period piece; they are spectators, and the history appears just as Shakespeare's Richard foretells it will, as a tale "of woeful ages long ago betid" (5.1.41–42). But the audience quickly become participants: the rebels in Richard's England enlist Shakespeare's sixteenth-century audience in their dangerous enterprise; the audience is made to share in their mistaken choices and participate in their crimes and errors.

By the time the audience learns, at the end of Act 2, scene 1, that the rebels have set sail from France to take Richard's throne, Shakespeare has shown Richard's personal faults and his inadequacy as a ruler so vividly that the audience is fully prepared to cheer for the rebels. It is as if the audience has been sucked back into the fourteenth century, deprived of its knowledge of the providential plan that would unfold only in subsequent years; thus confronted with the same situation that confronted their fourteenth-century ancestors, they make the same fatal choice against the true king and in favor of the usurper.

At the end of Act 3, just before the deposition scene, the audience is released from the characters' temporality by a curiously remote, self-consciously medieval tableau. In it, a gardener and his helper, speaking as no real gardeners can be imagined to speak, develop an elaborate allegorical argument condemning both Richard's dereliction of royal duties and Bolingbroke's unsurpation of Richard's divinely appointed throne.[16] The stylized unreality of the scene distances the audience from the characters' medieval time-situation and reminds them that what they are watching is a representation of an exemplary tale, a long-ago-completed action whose interpretation is not problematical but an established convention, and also that they have violated that convention in giving their allegiance to Bolingbroke. In the earlier scenes, the audience was made to share the characters' temporality and their action. Here action is reduced to stillness, and the characters' temporality recedes into a distant perspective where the audience no longer participates but simply observes. The characters are utterly stereotypical and inhuman, the faceless speakers of conventional judgments couched in conventional terms. Everything is, as it were, told in the past tense; no choices are possible because no choices remain to be made.

In a literal sense as well, no choices remain to be made. Richard, we learn in the garden scene, is about to be deposed; and in the next scene, we will see that deposition, the central historical event in the play. Everything in the play hinges on that scene: in it, the entire action—what is to come as well as what is past—is encapsulated; and in it is depicted an event so momentous and with such far-reaching consequences and paradigmatic significance that the Tudor historians of subsequent reigns repeatedly advert to it and Queen Elizabeth's censors, two centuries later, will feel the need to excise it from Shakespeare's play.

Shakespeare makes the deposition scene paradigmatic in his play as well, for in it he erases temporality altogether. In the garden scene, he showed the past as a historical tableau, remote and distant and informed by later historical judgments, thus insisting upon the audience's temporal separation from the action. In the earlier scenes, he made his audience share his characters' temporal situation and their fatally mistaken choice to depose Richard. In the deposition scene, the audience is made to reenact that choice and suffer the awareness of its consequences, not from the limited perspective of the fourteenth century, not from the remote and equally, although differently, limited perspective of their own temporal situation, but under the aspect of eternity. The audience is no longer locked in time but caught even more irrevocably in an endlessly present eternity of betrayal and guilt.

No sooner has the deposition been accomplished than the audience is made to suffer a terrible recognition. Northumberland demands that Richard read a confession of his crimes so that "the souls of men may deem that [he is] worthily depos'd" (4.1.226–27), but neither Richard nor Shakespeare is willing to have Richard read it, for the souls the rebels would satisfy include all those who have assembled to see the deposition—Shakespeare's sixteenth-century audience as well as Richard's fourteenth-century subjects—and the dialogue that follows is designed to condemn the deposition, not to justify it. Instead of reading the confession, Richard turns on his tormentor and reminds him of his own guilt, "mark'd with a blot, damn'd in the book of heaven," for deposing a rightful king. Then he broadens the indictment:

> Nay, all of you that stand and look upon me
> Whilst that my wretchedness doth bait myself,
> Though some of you, with Pilate, wash your hands,
> Showing an outward pity, yet you Pilates
> Have here deliver'd me to my sour cross,
> And water cannot wash away your sin.
>
>   (4.1.237–42)

In these lines, Richard implicates all of those who "stand and look upon" him, the audience in the theater as well as the characters on the stage, in the crime against the king that replicates the paradigmatic crime of the crucifixion.

The implication becomes stronger in the lines that follow. At first, Richard claims that he cannot read the account of his crimes because he is weeping: "Mine eyes are full of tears, I cannot see" (4.1.244). But the water image associates Richard with the rest of the traitors—all Pilates, all trying to wash away their guilt. Moreover, when Richard finally acknowledges his guilt, his self-indictment also implicates the audience. Richard says, "I find myself a traitor with the rest; / For I have given here my soul's consent / T'undeck the pompous body of a king; / Made glory base, [and] sovereignty a slave; / Proud majesty a subject, state a peasant" (4.1.248–52). Like Richard, and like the usurpers, the members of the audience have given their souls' consent to the deposition they stood and looked upon. Like Richard and the usurpers, they have made glory base and proud majesty a subject to their rebellious desires.

The words Richard uses to describe the guilt he shares with his spectators—"For I have given here my soul's consent"—insist upon the presence of the action. Time and space have collapsed, uniting the "here" of Richard's medieval court with the "here" of Shakespeare's sixteenth-century theater. Like the crucifixion scenes in medieval drama evoked by Richard's references to his "sour cross" and "you Pilates," the deposition erases the temporal distance between the outrageous historical event it depicts and the guilty contemporary audience that has come to see it enacted.

Unlike those medieval crucifixions, however, Richard's deposition, which takes place in Act 4, does not end the play; and in Act 5 Shakespeare will use a variety of strategies, including the most outrageous farce, to distance the audience from the action and restore them to their own time and place in a sixteenth-century theater. The grand poetry of the earlier parts of the play gives way to doggerel, and the sublime metaphors of royal state and cosmic significance are replaced by homely images of riding boots and beggars and the weary knees of an old man. The Duke of York, earlier presented as a dignified, eloquent spokesman for a nation and an audience torn by tragically divided loyalties, is now degraded to a caricature who wrangles with his wife in ridiculous rhymed couplets and ludicrously mixed metaphors in a frantic effort to insure that his own son will be executed for treason (5.3).

York's transformation is depicted in the most anachronistic speech in the entire play, where York develops an extended comparison between the history of the fourteenth century and the theater of Shakespeare's own time:

> As in a theatre the eyes of men,
> After a well-graced actor leaves the stage,
> Are idly bent on him that enters next,
> Thinking his prattle to be tedious,
> Even so, or with much more contempt, men's eyes
> Did scowl on gentle Richard. No man cried "God save him!"
> No joyful tongue gave him his welcome home,
> But dust was thrown upon his sacred head,
> Which with such gentle sorrow he shook off,
> His face still combating with tears and smiles,
> The badges of his grief and patience,
> That had not God, for some strong purpose, steel'd
> The hearts of men, they must perforce have melted,
> And barbarism itself have pitied him.
> But heaven hath a hand in these events,
> To whose high will we bound our calm contents.
> To Bullingbrook are we sworn subjects now,
> Whose state and honor I for aye allow.

(5.2.23–40)

The speech begins in eloquent blank verse that describes Bolingbroke's triumphal entry into London with Richard at his heels and ex-
presses York's sympathetic compassion for Richard, and it ends in stiff
rhymed couplets that declare his new allegiance to Bolingbroke and
reveal his own reduction from character to caricature. But even in the
earlier eloquent and compassionate portion of the speech, York is already distanced from the audience. He compares Bolingbroke to a
"well-graced actor" leaving the stage in a theater and Richard to an in-
ferior actor "that enters next" to be greeted with contempt by the theater audience. Thus, the procession that York describes reverses both
the historical action and the theatrical action Shakespeare's audience
has seen. Henry IV is following Richard II, not preceding him, as king
of England, and the king preferred by the verdict of the Tudor historians is Richard and not Henry. Moreover, Richard is also the "well-
graced actor" in Shakespeare's theater. Richard's is the leading role in
the play: no acting company would give the smaller and less demanding role of Bolingbroke to its best actor and deny him the chance to
play Richard. York's anachronistic comparison provides the final ad-
justment in the audience's perspective on the action: alienated from
the action on stage, first by York's reminder that they are in fact "in a
theatre" and that their judgments, informed by historical hindsight,
are more reliable than his, and then by the extravagantly farcical
scenes that follow this speech, the audience can withdraw from com-
plicity in Bolingbroke's rebellion and applaud the reassuring pieties
with which the play ends. Bolingbroke's own final judgment on Richard's murderer— "the guilt of conscience take thee for thy labor"—
rendered in the course in a series of comfortably conventional couplets (5.6.38–52) does not implicate the audience. Reiterating the familiar judgment of Tudor historians, it reestablishes the temporal distance between medieval court and Elizabethan theater and allows the
members of the audience to leave that theater restored to their own
time and place.

By confronting his audience with two temporal perspectives, each
of which insists upon the limitations of the other, Shakespeare makes
history disturbingly problematic. He also implies, however, that a
theater audience has a privileged vision of the past—a better understanding even than the characters who participated in the events he
portrays. Making the past present is not enough, for the characters in-

volved in the historical events, caught in their own temporality, had their own limitations of vision. The playwright, however, has the freedom to manipulate and transcend time to present the past under a variety of temporal perspectives and under the aspect of a self-consciously fictive analogue to the medieval historians' vision of eternity—a neutral zone outside of time where past and present can come together.

In the Henry IV plays, for instance, Shakespeare confronts his historical characters with the denizens of the Boar's Head Tavern—a real tavern in sixteenth-century London (Hemingway 124–25)—who live in a world outside of time. The king of that world is Falstaff, and the first words we ever hear from Falstaff are a question about the time of day. That question, however, is only an occasion for the prince's witty (and Shakespeare's usefully expository) demonstration that Falstaff has nothing to do with time:

What a devil hast thou to do with the time of the day? unless hours were cups of sack, and minutes capons, and clocks the tongues of bawds, and dials the signs of leaping-houses, and the blessed sun himself a fair hot wench in flame-color'd taffata; I see no reason why thou shouldst be so superfluous to demand the time of the day. (1.2.6–12)

In Falstaff's world, the historical prince meets unhistorical characters who drink anachronistic cups of sack and wear anachronistic ruffs and peach-colored silk stockings. There is even a man called Pistol—a character whose very name is an anachronism and whose speech is stitched together from scraps of plays that were not written until the sixteenth century for a theater that did not even exist at the time of Henry IV.[17]

Without the world of Falstaff, the audience cannot understand the world of Henry IV. Throughout the two plays, Shakespeare uses the comic plot to comment upon the historical action and the comic scenes to draw the audience into Hal's world.[18] And at the very end of the second play, it is Pistol, the most fantastic and anachronistic character of all, who delivers the most important historical message in the play.

Henry IV is not really the hero of the plays that bear his name. Enigmatic with the inscrutability of history itself, he reveals no motives or affections that are not directly involved with the affairs of state (and very few of those).[19] It is Prince Hal who forms the human and dramatic center of both the Henry IV plays. As Henry IV says on his deathbed, all his reign has been a kind of prologue for Hal's (4.5.197–99). Like the deposition of Richard II, the coronation of Henry V is the most anticipated dramatic event, as well as the most significant historical event, depicted in the play. Throughout the two Henry IV plays, the audience is led to anticipate the moment when Hal will throw off his loose behavior and shine forth in sunlike majesty as the mirror of all Christian kings celebrated by the English historians.

When that moment finally arrives, Falstaff, wasting time as usual, is off in Gloucestershire with an anachronistic justice named Shallow in Shakespeare's play but identified by modern scholars with various actual justices who lived in Shakespeare's neighborhood in the second half of the sixteenth century (Shaaber 637–44). Pistol rushes in, bursting with theatrical clichés and scraps of dialogue from old plays and frantic to deliver a message; but no one can tell what that message is because Pistol will not speak plain English. So far, the other characters have been speaking a plain, colloquial prose, but Falstaff finally breaks into a blank verse as stagey as Pistol's own to demand, "O base Assyrian knight, what is thy news? / Let King Cophetua know the truth thereof" (5.3.101–02). Then, at last, having been questioned in the anachronistic language of the sixteenth-century stage, Pistol reveals his early fifteenth-century news—that Henry IV is dead and Hal is now King Henry V.

That Shakespeare chooses such a blatantly theatrical and anachronistic character to carry this great historical message makes for a good joke, but it also serves as a paradigm for his method in the history plays. The historical record, like the inscrutable Henry IV or the enigmatic Henry V or the choral voice that interrupts Henry V's play, fails to communicate the human motives and actual life that lay behind the historic events. The human participants in those events had no way of knowing the consequences their actions would have in the future or of understanding their significance under the aspect of eternity. Shakespeare's manipulations of time explore those limitations, but they also exploit the temporal fluidity of his stage to offer his audience an analogue—self-consciously fictive and theatrical—of history as only God was privileged to see it, in general and in particular, in time and in eternity, present as living human action and also defined within the context of the future and a grand providential plan.[20]

Notes

[1]Ben Jonson, of course, did worry. See Herford and Simpson, 1:138.

[2]See Burckhardt's brilliant argument (4–11) that the clock in *Julius Caesar* is a deliberate anachronism, designed to signify to the audience that (9) "time is now reckoned in a new, Caesarean style." Although I am not entirely convinced by Burckhardt's interpretation of the clock's significance, his argument that the anachronism is deliberate has been an important influence on my thinking in this paper.

[3]Many writers make this point, but Levy, Burke, Fussner, and Greene are especially helpful.

[4]On sixteenth-century English efforts to draw distinctions between history and poetry, see Ferguson 28–38, "The Problem of Classification: History and Poetry," and Nelson 38–55.

[5]See Burke 1–2, 39–58; Levy 291 et passim; and Greene passim. Ebeling suggests (120–21) that the modern usage of the word "anachronism" derives from Scaliger's *De Emendiatione Temporum* (1583).

[6]Note that Cinthio associates the poet's obligation to use anachronisms with his obligation to be faithful to his present audience, unlike the writers who deplored anachronism, who argued that the poet was responsible for reporting the past accurately. There seems to be a connection between conservatism (allegiance to the past) and the prohibition against anachronism as well as a connection between a playwright's willingness to engage in metadramatic references to a present audience and his willingness to use anachronisms.

[7]Campbell 201. Modern scholars disagree on the extent—in fact, even on the presence—of political allegory in the play, but even the Arden editor, Peter Ure, who minimizes the political allegory, comments on the significance of this anachronism (65n). For a brief (although not unbiased) summary of the controversy, see the Arden edition lvii–lxii.

[8]Anne Barton's eloquent description is worth quoting: "The Crucifixion . . . becomes almost frighteningly real in those plays in which Christ appeals directly from The Cross to the people standing about the pageant. . . . He speaks to those spectators gathered together at Golgotha who were actually responsible for His death, but also to fourteenth-century Christians. Moments like this illuminate and make manifest that marriage of time present with time past upon which the mysteries are based" (22–23).

[9]I am indebted to Cary Mazer for the Nashe quotation.

[10]For an early statement of the discrepancy between what the Chorus says and what the audience sees on stage, see Goddard. For recent, sensitive discussions of the rela-

tionship between the Chorus's descriptions and the represented action, see Blanpied and Erickson.

[11]The critical controversy goes back at least as far as Samuel Johnson (see Walter xii–xiv). For a variety of modern estimates, see Berman. For an eminently sensible response to the controversy, see Rabkin, who argues that, like the modern psychologist's duck-rabbit, Shakespeare's *Henry V* is designed to be radically ambiguous: Like viewers of the trick drawing, readers of *Henry V* "can switch from one reading to another with increasing rapidity," remembering "the rabbit while" they "see the duck," but never able to "experience [the] alternative readings at the same time" (295).

[12]This may very well explain the violent arguments among critics of antithetical persuasion—the Tillyard-Campbell school seeing the plays as apologies for the received version and the iconoclasts equally convinced that the plays are out to subvert the pieties. Both sides can find excellent evidence because evidence for both positions is plentifully present in the plays.

[13]Tillyard 289. Tillyard's entire discussion emphasizes the medievalism of the play. On the appeal to an audience of local color and the appearance of well-known historical figures in historical drama, see Lindenberger 105–06.

[14]This view of the history plays as dramatizations of the Tudor myth was vigorously espoused by Tillyard, Campbell, and a number of other scholars in the 1940s and 1950s. In recent years, this conservative interpretation has been attacked by writers who have argued not only that Shakespeare did not endorse the Tudor myth but also, in some cases, that the Tudor myth itself was a figment of Tillyard's imagination. See especially Ornstein, Kelly, and Smith. For the purposes of this study, I am assuming that the Tudor myth did indeed exist but by no means in the univocal or uncritical form that Tillyard and his followers describe, that in this as in most matters the Elizabethans were probably just as capable as we are, not only of disagreeing with each other but also of being ambivalent, and that in any event, Shakespeare's history plays not only allow for ambivalence but require it and incite it if it did not exist before. Cf. Montrose, especially 54. For opposing views of the play's political significance for the Elizabethans, see Ure 1vii–1xii and Campbell 168–212.

[15]For an expanded version of my discussion of the role of the audience in *Richard II*, see Rackin. Those points where the role of the audience and the issue of temporality intersect are incorporated here.

[16]The allegory comparing the kingdom to a garden together with the queen's reference to the gardener as "old Adam's likeness" (3.4.73–76) brings up the traditional topos of the garden of Eden. Note that this scene, then, like the deposition scene, alludes to medieval mystery cycles and also to providential history, the kind of history that is not bound by the ordinary limits of time. The interesting difference is that the deposition scene implicates the audience while this scene distances them. I think this might have something to do with the subject. Eden is "Other" not only because of its remoteness in time but also because it deals with an unfallen state from which fallen humanity is necessarily excluded and because it deals with a world that is still, in a very important sense, timeless, since it is a world in which there is no such thing as death. The crucifixion, on the other hand, the topos invoked in the deposition scene, does involve its audi-

ence (note that Anne Barton uses a crucifixion scene to illustrate audience involvement in medieval drama), not only because all Christians are both guilty of and beneficiaries of Christ's crucifixion but also because it depicts a sinful act, one that the human imagination can comprehend in a way that it cannot comprehend a state of perfect innocence. Thus, although both the garden scene and the crucifixion scene contain allusions to both medieval drama and biblical history—i.e., ahistorical allusions—the garden scene is characterized as past, while the deposition scene is characterized as present. We think of the garden of Eden as being in the past—pastness is an essential quality of Eden. The crucifixion, on the other hand, like most events in biblical history, had the potentiality—indeed, the tendency—to seem eternally present.

[17]On the sack, see Hemingway 174; on the ruffs and peach-colored silk stockings, see Byrne 191–92. For an excellent brief discussion of Pistol, see Barton 140–43.

[18]This point has become a commonplace, but see Brooks and Heilman's early full demonstration (376–87) and Calderwood's provocative treatment (68–104).

[19]Even in his long soliloquy in Part 2 (3.1.1–31), alone on the stage in the middle of the night, dressed in his nightgown, the closest Henry can come to a personal reflection is to complain in generalized terms about the cares of kingship.

[20]Earlier versions of this paper were presented at the 1986 Ohio Shakespeare Conference and at the May 1986 meeting of the New York Shakespeare Society. I have profited greatly from the stimulating questions and suggestions offered on both those occasions.

Works Cited

BARTON, ANNE. *Shakespeare and the Idea of the Play.* London: Chatto and Windus, 1962.

BERMAN, RONALD, ed. *Twentieth Century Interpretations of Henry V.* Englewood Cliffs, NJ: Prentice-Hall, 1968.

BLANPIED, JOHN. *Time and the Artist in Shakespeare's English Histories.* Newark: U of Delaware P, 1983.

BROOKS, CLEANTH, and ROBERT B. HEILMAN. *Understanding Drama.* New York: Holt, 1948.

BURCKHARDT, SIGURD. *Shakespearean Meanings.* Princeton: Princeton UP, 1968.

BURKE, PETER. *The Renaissance Sense of the Past.* London: Edward Arnold, 1969.

BYRNE, M. ST. CLARE. "The Social Background." *A Companion to Shakespeare Studies.* Ed. Harley Granville-Barker and G. B. Harrison. New York: Doubleday, 1960.

CALDERWOOD, JAMES L. *Metadrama in Shakespeare's Henriad: Richard II to Henry V.* Berkeley: U of California P, 1979.

CAMPBELL, LILY B. *Shakespeare's "Histories": Mirrors of Elizabethan Policy.* San Marino: Huntington Library, 1947.

CASTELVETRO, LODOVICO. *A Commentary on the Poetics of Aristotle.* Trans. Allen H. Gilbert. *Literary Criticism: Plato to Dryden.* Ed. Allen H. Gilbert. Detroit: Wayne State UP, 1962.

CINTHIO, GIRALDI. *On the Composition of Romances.* Trans. Allen H. Gilbert. *Literary Criticism: Plato to Dryden.* Ed. Allen H. Gilbert. Detroit: Wayne State UP, 1962.

EBELING, HERMAN L. "The Word 'Anachronism.' " *MLN* 52 (1937): 120–21.-

ERICKSON, PETER B. " 'The Fault / My Father Made': The Anxious Pursuit of Heroic Fame in Shakespeare's *Henry V.*" *Modern Language Studies* 10 (1979–80): 10–25.

EVANS, G. BLAKEMORE, et al., eds. *The Riverside Shakespeare.* Boston: Houghton, 1974.

FERGUSON, ARTHUR B. *Clio Unbound: Perception of the Social and Cultural Past in Renaissance England.* Durham: Duke UP, 1979.

FUSSNER, F. SMITH. *The Historical Revolution: English Historical Writing and Thought 1580–1640.* London: Routledge and Kegan Paul, 1962.

_____. *Tudor History and the Historians.* New York and London: Basic, 1970.

GODDARD, HAROLD C. *The Meaning of Shakespeare.* Chicago: U of Chicago P, 1951.

GREENE, THOMAS. *The Light in Troy: Imitation and Discovery in Renaissance Poetry.* New Haven: Yale UP, 1982.

HALL, EDWARD. *The Union of the Two Noble and Illustre Famelies of Lancastre and Yorke.* 1548. London: J. Johnson et al., 1809.

HEMINGWAY, SAMUEL BURDETT, ed. *A New Variorum Edition of Henry the Fourth Part I.* Philadelphia: Lippincott, 1936.

JOHNSON, SAMUEL. Preface to *Shakespeare. Critical Theory Since Plato.* Ed. Hazard Adams. New York: Harcourt, 1971.

JONSON, BEN. "Conversations with Drummond." *Ben Jonson.* Ed. C. H. Herford and Percy Simpson. Vol. 1. Oxford: Clarendon, 1925. 138.

KELLY, HENRY ANSGAR. *Divine Providence in the England of Shakespeare's Histories.* Cambridge: Harvard UP, 1970.

LEVY, F. J. *Tudor Historical Thought*. San Marino: Huntington Library, 1967.

LINDENBERGER, HERBERT. *Historical Drama: The Relation of Literature and Reality*. Chicago: U of Chicago P, 1975.

MONTROSE, LOUIS ADRIAN. "The Purpose of Playing: Reflections on a Shakespearean Anthropology." *Helios* ns 7 (1980): 51–74.

NASHE, THOMAS. *Pierce Penilesse, His Supplication to the Diuell*. 1592. *The Elizabethan Stage*. Ed. E. K. Chambers. Vol. 4. Oxford: Clarendon, 1923.

NELSON, WILLIAM. *Fact or Fiction: The Dilemma of the Renaissance Storyteller*. Cambridge: Harvard UP, 1973.

ORNSTEIN, ROBERT B. *A Kingdom for a Stage: The Achievement of Shakespeare's History Plays*. Cambridge: Harvard UP, 1972.

RABKIN, NORMAN. "Rabbits, Ducks, and *Henry V*." *Shakespeare Quarterly* 28 (1977): 279–96.

RACKIN, PHYLLIS. "The Role of the Audience in Shakespeare's *Richard II*." *Shakespeare Quarterly* 36 (1985): 262–81.

SHAABER, MATTHIAS, ed. *A New Variorum Edition of Henry the Fourth Part Two*. Philadelphia: Lippincott, 1940.

SMITH, GORDON ROSS. " 'Princes of Doltish Disposition': Philippe de Comines, *King John*, and *Troilus and Cressida*." *Indian Journal of Linguistics* 8 (1971): 1–36.

STYAN, J. L. *Shakespeare's Stagecraft*. Cambridge: Cambridge UP, 1971.

TASSO, TORQUATO. *Discourses on the Heroic Poem*. Trans. Allen H. Gilbert. *Literary Criticism: Plato to Dryden*. Ed. Allen H. Gilbert. Detroit: Wayne State UP, 1962.

TILLYARD, E. M. W. *Shakespeare's History Plays*. New York: Barnes, 1944.

URE, PETER, ed. The Arden Edition of Shakespeare's *King Richard II*. London: Methuen, 1961.

WALTER, JOHN H., ed. The Arden Edition of Shakespeare's *King Henry V*. London: Methuen, 1954.

The Crowd in Theater and the Crowd in History:Fuenteovejuna

ANGUS MacKAY AND GERALDINE McKENDRICK

LOPE DE VEGA'S play *Fuenteovejuna,* dating from the early seventeenth century and based on real events which took place in 1476, presents us with the image of a justified and exemplary rebellion by the oppressed against their tyrannical lord.[1] It is this image, coupled with other features of the drama, which no doubt accounts for the enduring attraction of the play over the years. Basically, the plot tells the story of a group hero, the decent people of Fuenteovejuna, who, goaded by the barbaric treatment inflicted on them by their lord, the *comendador mayor* of the military Order of Calatrava, Fernán Gómez de Guzmán, rose up in a "peasant fury" one April night, stormed the house of the *comendador,* and, after a fierce conflict, savaged him to death.

By almost all his actions the *comendador* reveals that he is a tyrant, disrupting the harmony which should characterize the relationship between lord and vassals, and continually abusing his authority by stepping beyond the bounds of what is legal. His main crime is that of arbitrary sexual enjoyment from which none of the women is safe, but in the course of attempting to fulfill his desires he also abuses the males

125

of the town and totally disregards those locals who, under him, constitute part of the urban authority or government. The rebellion, therefore, is justified. It is a rebellion in which *all* the people of Fuenteovejuna participate. Naturally, Lope peopled his "crowd" with individuals, but these individuals are transcended, and the generic crowd becomes the hero in a peculiarly convincing and dramatic way.[2] They act as one and, after the deed, they continue to act as one. What they have done is, of course, shocking, even if we, the audience, know that it is justified. Inevitably, therefore, the Catholic kings send a judge to Fuenteovejuna to determine who led the rising and who is responsible. But when putting his questions, even under torture inflicted on women and children, the only answer he gets is: "Fuenteovejuna did it."

> JUDGE
> That boy!
> Tighter, dog, I know
> that you know. Tell who it was!
> Keeping quiet? Tighter, you drunk.

> BOY
> Fuenteovejuna, sir.[3]

The dramatic crowd not only acts as one but it provides its own justifications with the result that the "peasant fury" of the play is replete with disciplined, structured actions. The cry of ";Fuenteovejuna!," for example, is accompanied by the fundamental justification of the rebellion which consists of a combination of what may be termed "naïve monarchism" and the accusation of tyranny leveled against the *comendador* and his men.[4] This is a combination which is repeated many times:

> MENGO
> Long live the kings, our
> lords!

> ALL
> Long may they live!

> MENGO
> Death to tyrannical traitors!

ALL
Death to treacherous tyrants![5]

To this fundamental justification, however, two others of lesser importance should be added. In the first place, the "naïve monarchism" is to some extent linked to a wider "national" perspective, the actions taking place within a historical context in which the *comendador* is depicted as treacherously aiding the Portuguese enemy against the legitimate monarchs, Ferdinand and Isabella. Secondly, the *comendador* and his men are repeatedly depicted as "bad Christians" as well as tyrants, an accusation which, as will be seen, is not without its significance:

ALL
Fuenteovejuna! Long live King Ferdinand!
Death to bad Christians and traitors![6]

Of course it would be idle to pretend that a great deal of the play was not the product of Lope de Vega's dramatic imagination. His Fuenteovejuna is, as a place, characterized by an idealized and primitive arcadian harmony, and its honorable peasants are unconvincingly capable of debating learned and metaphysical problems in homely rustic speech.[7] This harmony/honor is violently overturned by the evil *comendador,* and it is only by the counterviolence of rebellion that harmony/honor is restored. It has been argued, and rightly so, that Lope de Vega marked each of these three stages with important ritualistic ceremonies. In Act 1, when the people of Fuenteovejuna welcome their *comendador* in a ritualistic manner on his entry into the town, the ceremony emphasizes the harmony that should prevail between a lord and his subjects. In Act 2 a wedding ceremony, once again ritualistically emphasizing the harmony that should prevail among the people of Fuenteovejuna, is violently interrupted by the *comendador* who puts an end to the festivities and carries off the wedding couple by force. Finally, in Act 3, the ritualistic acts of the crowd, terminating in the murder of the comendador, mark the transition to a situation of harmony/honor restored.[8]

The play, then, has a dramatic and group hero, the crowd, and this crowd acts in a structured and ordered way with justifications for resorting to what Natalie Davis would call "The Rites of Violence." But since

Lope de Vega based his play on a historical episode which took place in 1476, several intriguing questions arise. Did "the crowd in history" act in the same way as the ordered "crowd in the play"? Were the rituals of violence in 1476 as prevalent as in Lope's creation? In short, was the historical crowd as dramatic and ritualistic as the fictional crowd?

There are two important narrative accounts of the events which took place in Fuenteovejuna during the late night and early morning of the 22–23 of September 1476. In his *Crónica de las tres órdenes de Santiago, Calatrava y Alcántara* Rades y Andrada provided the material from which Lope de Vega drew the essential elements for his play. But, whereas for Rades the *comendador* was undoubtedly a tyrant, Alonso de Palencia in his *Crónica de Enrique IV* depicted him as a kind and generous lord who even visited the sick of Fuenteovejuna.[9] According to Palencia the only complaint that could be leveled against the *comendador* would seem to be one relating to an increase in taxes.[10] However, although diametrically opposed in their sympathies, both Rades and Palencia are in substantial agreement as to what happened during the uprising. In addition to these two narrative accounts it is of course necessary to bear in mind documentation which relates more or less indirectly to the events in question and to other episodes of a similar nature.

As for Fuenteovejuna itself it is difficult to categorize its inhabitants as either peasants or townsmen.[11] Certainly with its 985 *vasallos,* that is some 4,500 inhabitants, it could hardly be described as a village. On the other hand its extensive pastoral lands, its location astride the sheepwalks of the Mesta, and its production of wool and honey made it more markedly rural than most of the other agro-towns of the region. In what follows, therefore, it must be remembered that, quite apart from the fact that rural society had its own hierarchies, these "peasants" lived within a context of institutions which were urban in nature. More important still, the annual revenues of Fuenteovejuna, amounting to some 80,000 *mrs,* attracted the attention of the great lords of the region, including above all the city of Cordoba.[12] To whom did Fuenteovejuna belong? This was the problem which in a significant way lay behind the uprising of 1476.

The later medieval period in the kingdom of Castile witnessed a flood of royal privileges or *mercedes* in favor of the great nobility, and among these *mercedes* the alienation of towns, previously belonging to the lordships and jurisdictions of the larger royal cities, figured prominently. It was in this way that Cordoba, which was especially affected by these alienations, lost Fuenteovejuna. Already in the 1450s the city of Cordoba and the inhabitants of Fuenteovejuna had been involved, along with others, in resisting the depredations of the great lords, particularly the master of the Order of Alcántara. Then in 1460 Henry IV granted the towns of Fuenteovejuna and Bélmez to Pedro Girón, who also happened to be master of the Order of Calatrava. Girón, faced with the certainty of a tenacious opposition on the part of the Cordoban authorities, entered into a series of complicated transactions by means of which Fuenteovejuna and Bélmez, which had been granted to him as an individual, were eventually exchanged with Osuna and Cazalla, which belonged to the military order of which he was master. In this way the conflict with Cordoba over the jurisdiction and lordship of Fuenteovejuna and Bélmez was off-loaded four years later on to the Order of Calatrava. Despite the resistance of Cordoba, therefore, Fuenteovejuna had become an *encomienda mayor* of the Order by 1464, and by 1468–69 the *comendador mayor* of Calatrava, Fernán Gómez de Guzmán, had established his headquarters in the town.[13] The latter, of course, was the "tyrant" who was murdered in the "peasant fury" of 1476.

Like Lope de Vega's crowd, the rebels of 1476 thought that their actions were legitimate and, far from displaying guilt, they rejoiced at the outcome of their violence. Indeed they acted not only as if they were, in some sense, royal agents but as if as a collectivity they had the right, in these specific circumstances, of correcting defective government or, at the very least, of executing proper royal policies. But how could they justify themselves when, on the face of it, Fuenteovejuna had legally passed into the possession of the Order of Calatrava and its commander, Fernán Gómez de Guzmán? As we shall see, "the crowd" was not, as Palencia would have us believe, simply a base rabble or "furious multitude" (*furiosa multitud*). It included, or was influenced by, men of substance, both in Fuenteovejuna and Cordoba itself. Although not all the participants in the uprising would appreciate all the justifications for the violence and murder, all of them would be aware of at least some of the justifications. What were these?

At the most theoretical-practical level there was, astonishingly for the kingdom of Castile, the notion of a solemn pact or contract. The notion seems anachronistic because Castilian kings during the fifteenth century, and in particular John II (1406–54), had largely succeeded in establishing that they were above the law, held their power directly from God, and had at their disposal a form of "absolute royal power."[14] Yet this trend in the increase of the monarch's theoretical powers had not been without its setbacks. In particular the *cortes* of Valladolid of 1442 had grasped the opportunity presented to them when John II fell temporarily into the hands of his noble opponents. And in effect the very first petition of this *cortes* established a solemn pact (*pacto*), contract (*contracto*), and law (*ley*) between the king and his subjects concerning the very kind of royal privileges of alienation which had affected Cordoba and Fuenteovejuna.[15] The *procuradores* reminded the king that "during the last ten years your majesty has given away certain villages, towns, and places belonging to other cities and towns, and you have divided them off and separated them from [these cities and towns] in order to give them away, by means of which the said cities and towns have been greatly affronted and damaged."[16] By the solemn pact and contract (*pacçion e contracto*) such grants were, with very minor exceptions, to cease, and both John II and his successors were to be bound by the pact or contract, notwithstanding any future use of the Crown's absolute royal power to the contrary. If any kings should fail to observe the contract, then those subjects who were affected by any such royal privilege could "organise real or verbal resistance of any kind that can be envisaged, even if it is by an affray with armed men, and notwithstanding whether such a privilege or grant is carried into effect or not."[17] More specifically it was stated that "the inhabitants of such cities and towns and places and castles can, on their own authority and without any punishment, return to the lordship of the royal crown of your kingdoms at any time, and can resist by force of arms, or by any other means, the person to whom such a privilege might be granted."[18] Clearly, by the terms of this pact or contract, Henry IV's alienation of Fuenteovejuna had been illegal, and the rebels' right to organize an uprising against the *comendador mayor* was legally sanctioned.

All the circumstantial evidence suggests that some of the rebels of 1476 were probably aware of this right to resort to arms. At the very least two points are abundantly clear. Firstly, if during the night's events the crowd did not actually know that their actions could be interpreted as a legitimate attempt to restore Fuenteovejuna to the royal city of Cordoba, and thus to the Crown, then this legitimation was, as we shall see, immediately adopted in a ritualistic way on the morrow of the *comendador*'s murder. Secondly, the authorities of Cordoba, who were implicated in the revolt, had for long been aware of the right to use force and had in fact manipulated political events in order to have this right confirmed.[19] In the divisions resulting from the attempted deposition-in-effigy of Henry IV in 1465, for example, the Order of Calatrava had largely sided with the king's enemies, and the city of Cordoba had seized its chance to obtain royal approval to regain lost territory, including Fuenteovejuna, by force: "because we order all of you, and each and every one of you, to join together and go to the said places and their lands . . . and enter, take, and empower yourselves in them . . . for me and for the Crown of my kingdoms and for that said city of Cordoba."[20] Ten years later an even more wide-ranging confirmation was obtained from Queen Isabella, who not only promised both to restore to Cordoba all those lands and places which had been illegally alienated and to annul all future alienations, but also guaranteed the right of the inhabitants of these areas "to rise up and rebel on our behalf and on behalf of our royal Crown without receiving or incurring any pain or punishment as a result."[21]

The evidence relating to the events of the night of 22 September indicates that there were further grounds for the legitimation of violence. Although, unlike Lope, Rades does not actually use the word "tyrant," his description of the *comendador*'s actions makes it clear that they constituted tyrannical behavior which, by entailing *maltratamiento* and an arbitrary disregard for the persons and property of the people of Fuenteovejuna, legitimated rebellion. In addition the *comendador*, according to Rades, was providing military support for the king of Portugal against the Catholic kings, and thus the rebels' "monarchism" and their cry of "Death to the traitors!," far from being "naïve," constituted a political stance which justified their violence:

That knight had perpetrated *maltratamiento* on his vassals, having many soldiers in the town to support the king of Portugal, who claimed to be king of Castile. And he allowed these overbearing soldiers to commit serious outrages and affronts to the people of Fuenteovejuna, eating up their wealth. In addition to this, the *comendador mayor* himself had inflicted great outrages and infamies on those of the town, taking their daughters and wives by force, and robbing them off their wealth, in order to maintain those soldiers which he had . . . [22]

Finally, although Rades does not explain why, the rebels also considered the *comendador* and his men to be "bad Christians" (*malos Christianos*). Such a charge during this period immediately suggests hostility toward New Christians (*conversos*), but in fact there is no evidence that Fernán Gómez was a *converso,* and recent research has shown that the explanation is more straightforward. For some time Fernán Gómez had been at odds with the ecclesiastical authorities of Cordoba over revenues and properties in Fuenteovejuna and Bélmez. Not only had he usurped the tithes of these areas, but he had prevented the canons of Cordoba cathedral from taking possession of lands and properties which had been bequeathed to them by one of their recently deceased colleagues, Fernán Ruiz de Aguayo. The upshot was that not only were the *comendador* and his supporters excommunicated, but also both Fuenteovejuna and Bélmez were subjected to an interdict. Thus, shortly before the uprising, the actions of the "bad Christians," that is Fernán Gómez and his men, had affected all the people of Fuenteovejuna inasmuch as all church services, apart from the baptism of infants and penance for the dying, had been suspended.[23]

The existence of these sophisticated justifications for the use of legitimate violence makes it impossible to accept the view, implied by Palencia, that the actions of the rebel crowd were the irrational, almost meaningless, manifestations of a crazed and chaotic bunch of savages. It is true, as we shall see, that Palencia did credit the crowd with some planning and organization, and he does mention that an increase in taxes constituted a pretext for the violence, but essentially he saw the crowd as a "*furiosa multitud,*" made up of "ferocious peasants" (*feroces rústicos*) who lurked menacingly in the woodlands, and whose iniquitous actions were rendered all the more violent by the fact that hunting had endowed them with "savage habits" (*hábitos feroces*). And, inevitably, Palencia maintains that after the crazed bloodletting, the crowd turned to pillaging: "Afterwards they took the gold, silver, and other items of wealth, and they became enraged with the *comendador*'s servants, who had been their friends."[24]

In fact the crowd was highly organized. For a start the people of Fuenteovejuna had planned the uprising. Both Rades and Palencia are agreed on this point. According to Rades, "all of them with one will and accord decided to rise up against [the *comendador*] and kill him," while Palencia states that Fernán Gómez's fate was planned at "secret meetings" and "illegal reunions."[25] Further, both chroniclers are agreed that the people of Fuenteovejuna had formed themselves into a sworn association. Palencia merely refers to "the wicked sworn conspiracy of those of Fuenteovejuna," but Rades, when accounting for the subsequent failure of the royal judge to obtain information, asserts emphatically that "they were in a sworn association."[26] In fact by entering into such an association the people of Fuenteovejuna had resorted to a traditional form of organization which had characterized other similar episodes in medieval Castile, including the *hermandades,* and which would be highly influential in the Revolt of the Comuneros of 1520.[27] In 1296 in Cuenca, for example, all the town's inhabitants, like those of Fuenteovejuna, entered into a sworn association, "all as one," in order to remain a royal town, defend their laws (*fuero*), uphold justice, and prevent anyone powerful from "perpetrating wrong, force, dishonour, or arrogance."[28] Moreover, as Gutiérrez Nieto has pointed out with respect to the *comunidad* of Toledo in 1520, a sworn association had other distinct advantages apart from that of uniting opposition to a common enemy. In preparing for justified violence, leadership might well be provided by the town's council or *regimiento*. But however legitimate, violence was certain to be followed by reprisals, with the ringleaders receiving exemplary punishment. An alternative, therefore, was a sworn association which implicated all the inhabitants and made it clear that the town as a whole was resisting tyranny and injustice.[29] Indeed in the case of Fuenteovejuna, as we shall see, even the women and children participated in the rites of violence. The crowd, therefore, was Fuenteovejuna itself. It was this factor that led to the royal judge's failure to extract information, and it was also this factor which excited the admiration of both Rades and Lope de Vega. Rades makes his admiration manifest:

An examining judge came from the royal court to Fuenteovejuna, with a commission from the Catholic Kings, in order to find out the truth about the affair, and to punish the guilty. But even though he tortured many of those who had been present at the death of the *comendador mayor,* no one was ever willing to confess who were the captains and those responsible for that crime, nor would they give the names of those involved. The judge asked them: "Who killed the *comendador mayor?*" They replied: "Fuenteovejuna." He asked them: "Who is Fuenteovejuna?" They replied: "All the inhabitants of this town." In the end all the replies were the same, because they had sworn an oath that, even if he should torture them to death, they would give the same reply. And what is more to be admired is that the judge had torture applied to many women and very young youths, and they displayed the same constancy and spirit as the strongest of the men.[30]

The existence of a sworn association meant, of course, that the social composition of the crowd was not, as Palencia would have us believe, simply one of *"feroces rústicos."* In fact, as Rades makes clear, everyone participated in one way or another in the violence that was perpetrated that night. To begin with, the initial attack involved the urban officers and oligarchs, as well as the *vecinos*: "the *alcaldes, regidores,* judicial officials and council joined together with the other inhabitants and, armed, they forced their way into the houses of the *encomienda mayor,* where the *comendador* was."[31] Then, after the *comendador* had been mortally wounded, but before he died, the women of Fuenteovejuna turned up with tambourines and rattles to celebrate the death of their lord. The children, too, turned up to solemnify the *comendador*'s murder. And all of them—men, women, and children—participated in the macabre rejoicings that subsequently took place in the square of Fuenteovejuna. Then, too, there were others who had participated indirectly. Historians have suspected, on the basis of convincing circumstantial evidence, that the oligarchs of Cordoba aided and abetted the preparations for the uprising.[32] Indeed Palencia alleges—and the allegation is by no means improbable—that Don Alonso de Aguilar, the greatest noble in the region and *alcalde mayor* of Cordoba, had sent messengers to Fuenteovejuna to incite rebellion.[33]

The existence of a sworn association and the assertions of those interrogated that the culprit was Fuenteovejuna as a united whole, however, did not imply that, for the occasion, the crowd had no structure or hierarchy. As has been seen, men, women, and children intervened in the violence at different times and in different ways. Moreover, we know from Rades that the children imitated their mothers: "The children also organised a company with its captain, in imitation of their mothers, and, arranged in the order that their age made possible, went to solemnify the said death." As for the women, "they had made . . . a flag, and had appointed a captain and lieutenant." Were the women, in turn, imitating the men? Rades, it will be remembered, described how those interrogated by the judge refused to confess who the "captains" were. In all probability, therefore, the rebels had their flag, their captains, and their lieutenants—a hierarchy and organization subsequently imitated by the women and children.[34] If this is the case, then the crowd was not dissimilar to an *hermandad* or *comunidad*—both of these organizations being characterized by, among other things, a sworn association, collective decision-making, and the existence of captains.[35] Thus in the *cortes* of Ocaña of 1422, for example, we find allegations of townspeople, led by *capitanes de comunidad,* rising up against the *alcaldes, regidores,* and other urban officials. Similarly, those participating in the *comunidad* of Baza of 1520 were accused of joining together in a sworn association in order to create a *comunidad,* with syndics and a captain, and to strip the *corregidor's* lieutenant of his staff of office.[36] In both the examples just cited the *común* was opposed to the urban authorities, and in such cases it was usual for the insurgents to elect alternative officials to replace them. The case of Fuenteovejuna was different: there was no *corregidor* and, as has been seen, the *regidores* and *alcaldes* participated in the sworn association. In other respects, however, there was little difference. Indeed, as will be seen, the people of Fuenteovejuna later performed the same rituals involving *varas* (staffs of office) and the reappointment of officials.

With a structured organization and justified objectives, the actions of the crowd of Fuenteovejuna during the night of violence made sense, despite the apparent chaos. This was made manifest by the *voz* or "cry." In late medieval Castile the *voz* was the oral equivalent of a flag or banner—that is, it subsumed, in highly "telegraphed" form, all those elements which signified what its supporters stood for. The *voz,* therefore, by implication revealed a policy or program, and as a matter of fact chroniclers often briefly explain the essential program signified by the *voz.* For example, Rades, while telling us that the *comendador* maintained the *voz* of the king of Portugal, immediately adds in explanation, "who claimed to be king of Castile."[37] Translated into direct speech, the *voz* of the people of Fuenteovejuna was: "Fuenteovejuna! Fuenteovejuna! Long live King Ferdinand and Queen Isabel! Death to the traitors and bad Christians!" ("¡Fuenteovejuna! ¡Fuenteovejuna! ¡Vivan los Reyes don Fernando y doña Isabel! ¡Mueran los traidores y malos cristianos!") This *voz* revealed their program. (a) *¡Fuenteovejuna! ¡Fuenteovejuna!* The crowd, made up of the people of Fuenteovejuna and organized as a sworn association, rose up collectively against the tyrannical *comendador*. Logically, when the roy'' judge later asked that the guilty persons be named, the invariable answer was: "Fuenteovejuna did it." (b) *¡Vivan los Reyes don Fernando y doña Isabel!* The crowd was supporting the Catholic kings against the king of Portugal and against those who, like Fernán Gómez, maintained the Portuguese king's *voz*. But in another sense the crowd was also acting as an extension of government, putting into effect what the monarchy should have done, indeed secretly wanted to do. Quite apart from the *comendador's* tyranny, Fuenteovejuna did not belong to him or to the Order of Calatrava—it belonged to the royal city of Cordoba and, hence, to the Crown. The subsequent actions of the rebels, as we shall see, revealed that they were conscious of this situation. Thus, during the crisis, they arrogated to themselves special powers in order to supplement royal authority and to act on behalf of the Crown. But, once the crisis was over, a whole new set of rituals would be put into operation to restore a "proper" and "harmonious" political order. (c) *¡Mueran los traidores y malos cristianos!* The traitors were, of course, those who maintained the *voz* of the king of Portugal, and the bad Christians were Fern'an G'omez and his men who had been excommunicated and who had caused Fuenteovejuna to be placed under an interdict.

The *voz* of the crowd presaged the gruesome way in which Fernán Gómez was to be killed and his corpse desecrated amid scenes of jubilation. According to Rades, the rebels stormed the headquarters of the *encomienda mayor* and, after killing fourteen men, finally reached Fernán Gómez, dealing him mortal wounds which left him stretched out, unconscious, on the floor. Before he died, however, they threw his body out of a window, and those below in the street caught the falling *comendador* on the points of their upturned lances and swords. These men then proceeded to tear out his beard and hair, and smash his teeth with the pummels of their swords. At this stage, and before Fernán Gómez finally expired, the women and children, with their captains, lieutenants, flags, and musical instruments, turned up to celebrate and "solemnify" the death of the *comendador*. Subsequently all the men, women, and children carried the body to the square of Fuenteovejuna amid great rejoicings, and "there all the men and women tore the corpse to pieces, dragging the body along the ground and perpetrating great cruelties and mocking insults to it."[38] Finally, as a culmination to these particular scenes, they refused to hand over the *comendador's* remains to his servants for burial. Palencia, with variations, tells a similar story. According to him the *comendador* was already dead, and the corpse already half destroyed, before the defenestration, the crowd below finishing off the process by ripping the body into pieces. Moreover he adds that an old woman who tried to collect the shapeless bits and pieces in a basket was whipped, while a Franciscan who wished to bury the remains was lucky to escape with his life.

Gruesome as these scenes were, they make sense. Obviously the *comendador's* house could not contain all the people of Fuenteovejuna, but the need for total participation was met by throwing Fernán Gómez to those who remained below in the street. Whether Rades is accurate about the precise moment of the *comendador's* death is not of vital importance. What was important was that all the people of Fuenteovejuna, including the women and children, should have been perceived as participating in some way in the ritual murder, and therefore before death occurred. Once again the actions transferred responsibility from individuals to the collectivity: "Fuenteovejuna did it."

But did the savage acts of violence inflicted on the body simply reflect a crazed fury or did they carry some symbolic or ritual meaning? It is difficult to ascribe any precise significance to the tearing out of the beard and hair, and the smashing of teeth, and the references to the "great cruelties" and "mocking insults" proferred to the corpse in the square are extremely vague. The beard and hair, of course, were symbolic of honor and virility, as is evidenced by the fact that the Cid prided himself that his beard had never been plucked, whereas that part of the beard which he had wrenched from the face of his enemy, García Ordoñez, had never grown properly again.[39] Given Fernán Gómez's sexual atrocities, therefore, the uprooting of his beard and hair could represent an attack on his virility, and it is by no means improbable that the "great cruelties" and "mocking insults" included the act of castration.

In more general terms, however, the torturing of the body, the desecration of the corpse, and the refusal to permit burial all point to the conclusion that the crowd was behaving in a quasi-official manner—that is, it was carrying out actions which properly belonged to the realm of *official* punishments. The savagery inflicted on the body of the traitor, Fernán Gómez, was no more appalling than that envisaged and approved of by Alfonso X in the law code of the *Siete Partidas*. The fate of the traitor, according to law, should be that "they kill him cruelly for it, dragging his body along the ground, or dismembering it, so that it be a warning to everyone not to do the same thing." Subjects, in fact, should give traitors "the strangest manner of death possible."[40] Alfonso X talked in terms of "dismembering" (*desmembrando*) and "dragging" (*rastrando*); Rades says that "they cut him into pieces, dragging him"(*le hizieron pedaços, arrastrandole*). Were the people of Fuenteovejuna not in fact accurately enacting what was envisaged in the *Siete Partidas?* What is more, the law fully backed up the crowd in its refusal to allow burial. Firstly, traitors could not be buried in the land of those whom they had betrayed: "For Holy Church did not think it fit that they should be buried in hallowed ground. On the contrary they ordered that if it was discovered that they were buried there, their bones should be taken out and scattered in the fields or burned. . . ."[41] Secondly, being excommunicated, Fernán Gómez could not be buried by the Church. Thirdly, because of the interdict no one in Fuenteovejuna could be properly buried.[42] Was the crowd, then, not acting on behalf of the lay and ecclesiastical authorities?

After the murder, the crowd continued to behave in an ordered and ritualistic manner. Rades partly hints at this:

After they had killed the *comendador mayor* the people of Fuenteovejuna removed the staffs and offices of justice from those who had been appointed by the Order, to whom the jurisdiction belonged, and gave them to whom they wished. Then they turned to the city of Cordoba and commended themselves to it, saying that they wanted to be in Cordoba's jurisdiction, as they had been before the town fell into the hands of Pedro Girón.[43]

In fact part of what Rades is here describing was the traditional ritual and symbolic behavior implicit in most such episodes, as is evidenced by the numerous examples during the revolt of the *Comuneros*. The removal of the *varas* or staffs of office by the people denoted that whoever the office-conferring authority had been, this authority was no longer recognized. Indeed, frequently these degradation ceremonies entailed no hostility to the persons of the officeholders, who would subsequently be reinstated.[44] Hence, since the officials in Fuenteovejuna had participated in the rising, it is highly likely that they had their staffs and offices restored to them by the people. Yet political order and harmony would not be fully reestablished until Cordoba's lordship had been visually, orally, and ritually restored.

In Lope de Vega's play, as has been noted, the transitions from harmony, to disharmony, and to harmony restored are marked by ritualistic episodes. In real life the restoration of harmony was accompanied by even more elaborate rituals. Fortunately these were considered to be so important that they were written down and described by notarial documents attested to by witnesses.[45]

At one level, of course, the people of Fuenteovejuna and the Cordoban authorities were anxious to confirm that they were simply obeying the commands of the Catholic kings, and to this end there was, naturally enough, much citing of royal letters. In addition, however, Fuenteovejuna was being restored to Cordoba, and the purpose of each ritual was to act as "a sign of the reintegration, restitution, and continuation" of Fuenteovejuna in the city's lordship. These rituals involved the symbolic appropriation of the urban space, rites of purification, and symbolic acts of jurisdiction. As in Lope's play, the theoretical objective was the restoration of harmony. Thus when Juan de Berrio, *alcalde mayor* of Cordoba, symbolically "began to hear and deal with legal cases" in Fuenteovejuna, "he gave it as his judgement that all should live in peace and concord."[46]

The Cordoban authorities were indeed remarkably quick to appear on the scene. By the morning of Monday 29 April their representatives, made up of two *alcaldes mayores,* three *regidores,* and one *procurador,* were already installed, along with the council and officials of Fuenteovejuna, in a monastery or hermitage near the town. Later the same day they moved to some taverns (*mesones*) just outside the town walls, and there then began the series of rituals which were to continue throughout the following day. As each episode took place, a public scribe (*escribano público*) was asked to produce testimonies for some or all of the leading participants. For the most part these were the Cordoban authorities, although those of Fuenteovejuna were not averse to asking for copies as well: "and each one of them in the name of the said lord council of the said city asked me, the said public scribe and notary, to give each one of them a public and written testimony, signed by me and bearing my sign."[47] Such documents, themselves the product of a form of ritual, also bore the names of witnesses to the events, and in some cases they reveal that the rites were performed to accompanying acclamations of confirmation by the people of Fuenteovejuna.

The rituals appropriating the urban space began on the Monday. The officials and people of Fuenteovejuna formally invited the Cordoban authorities to make an entry through the gate of the Cal Maestra. The doors of course had been shut on purpose, and the Cordoban officials ceremoniously opened them "as a sign of possession." They then entered to the enthusiastic rejoicings and shouts of the people of Fuenteovejuna: "Long live the king and queen, our lords, and lord Cordoba!"; "Cordoba! Cordoba! Cordoba!" Next day all the four town gates—those of the Corredera, San Sebastian, Cordoba, and the Cal Maestra—were, at different times, to be the *foci* of other rituals. Outside the San Sebastian gate, for example, the officials of Fuenteovejuna took the *procurador* of Cordoba, Pedro Rodríguez Cobo, by the hands, "and put him and placed him physically and on his feet inside the said town of Fuenteovejuna." In front of the assembled crowds Cobo then "walked physically and on foot within the said town along the street which is in front of the said San Sebastian gate, from some parts to others, and, being within, he locked the doors of the gate of the said town to the countryside, and then he opened them, being on the inside, all of which . . . he said . . . that he had done . . . as a sign of reintegration and restitution."[48] The ritual was similar with respect to all four gates, except that at the first one a key was ceremoniously handed over, and at the last gate *all* the Cordoban officials, and not just the *procurador,* carried out the ritual actions. Watched by the people, "Cordoba" had been placed bodily within the walls, "Cordoba" had walked in the streets of Fuenteovejuna, "Cordoba" had locked and opened the gates—the new lord was in town and Fuenteovejuna had been ritually invested.

Rituals of purification involved the removal of polluting elements associated with the recently murdered *comendador mayor.* Two of these elements, the pillory and the gallows, were the visible reminders of Fernán Gómez's exercise of lordship. When the crowd had celebrated their murder of the *comendador* by taking his body to the square and dismembering it, they had perhaps not acted unfortuitously, because it was in the square that the *comendador* had dispensed his form of justice and it was there, too, that the pillory was located. It was to this square that the officials from Cordoba and the crowds now repaired, and Pedro Rodríguez Cobo, on behalf of the city of Cordoba, symbolically removed some stones from the base of the pillory with his own hands, proclaiming that Cordoba ordered the pillory and its base to be removed and destroyed. And in effect the crowds returned at a later stage to watch another Cordoban official pull down the pillory, destroy it, and flatten the ground on which it had been erected. Meanwhile the gallows, which rested on three brick pillars outside the town walls, had been subjected to a similar ritual of destruction.[49] A third polluting element was more personal. Immediately after the final ritual at the gate of the Cal Maestra one of the Cordoban oligarchs "took a lance with his own hands and knocked down and destroyed the top of the inside wall, which is above the said gate of the Cal Maestra, where there were depicted some figures and arms, which are said to be the arms of the said *comendador mayor.* "[50]

Appropriating the urban space and destroying visual vestiges of the late *comendador's* person and his exercise of lordship, however, were not enough. Rituals were needed to establish that lord "Cordoba" now effectively administered judicial power in Fuenteovejuna. It was this need which explains the charming episodes involving fictitious lawsuits. In the square at Fuenteovejuna there was a stone bench or platform for the administration of justice. Inevitably, perhaps, the *procurador* of Cordoba sat on this bench in front of the crowds as "a sign of the reintegration and restitution" of Fuenteovejuna to the city's lordship. He was followed by Juan de Berrio, *alcalde mayor* of Cordoba, who "climbed up and sat himself on the said bench and tribunal and, as a sign of the said possession . . . and as *alcalde mayor* of the said city of Cordoba and its territory, and in the presence of the said people, began to hear and determine cases, and gave it as his verdict that everybody should be and live in peace and concord."[51] Visually, orally, and ritually, lord "Cordoba" had decided that harmony and law and order should be restored. Indeed so important was this rite that later, and once again in the presence of the crowds, it was repeated. After the privileges of Fuenteovejuna had been solemnly confirmed by the Cordoban officials in the church of Santa María, "then immediately on the said day, month, year, and hour, and in the presence of us, the said Gómez González and Gómez Fernández, public scribes and notaries, the said Juan de Berrio sat down on the said bench and tribunal as *alcalde mayor* in order to hear and determine cases, ratifying, using, and continuing the said possession. . . ."[52]

It is fortunate that descriptions of these rituals have survived. It is equally unfortunate that these written documents cannot properly convey the extent to which these rituals must have been extraordinarily rich in sensory references. When the *procurador* of Cordoba, representing the lord "Cordoba," walked up and down the streets of Fuenteovejuna, did he do this in a solemn and deliberate manner, amid silence, or did he walk gaily amid much rejoicing? What exactly were the mocking insults proferred to the corpse of Fernán Gómez in the square? We shall never know. But we can be certain that the persons, events, and rituals which have been considered constituted a vivid kind of language, the equivalent, perhaps, of Lévi-Strauss's *bonnes à penser*—that is, they were rituals with which to think. As for the events of the night of the uprising, they illustrated an even more important feature. To the questions put by a baffled judge, the reply had invariably been: "Fuenteovejuna did it." But in doing what they did the crowd demonstrated that the ritualistic and symbolic was not merely a reflection of political action—it constituted an essential part of it. In real life Fuenteovejuna had witnessed events and rituals which were every bit as dramatic and sophisticated as those which Lope de Vega subsequently presented on the stage.

Notes

[1]All citations from the play are from the edition by Francisco López Estrada. All translations from the play and from historical sources are our own.

[2]Larson 86: "For the first time in Lope, and for one of the first times in literature, we have in Fuenteovejuna a group hero."

3

> JUEZ
> ¡Ese muchacho!
> Aprieta, perro, yo sé
> que lo sabes. ¡Di quién fue!
> ¿Callas? Aprieta, borracho.
>
> NIÑO
> Fuente Ovejuna, señor.
>
> (2211–15)

4The expression "naïve monarchism" appears to have been first used by Blum 335. Its use here does not imply that the ideology, characterized by long-standing traditions and concepts of a proper social order, as well as appeals to the Crown, was necessarily a naïve phenomenon. Indeed Herrero has cogently argued that Lope's play is about the triumph of the monarchy and the people over the tyranny of feudalism.

5

> MENGO
> ¡Los reyes, nuestros señores, vivan!
>
> TODOS
> ¡Vivan muchos años!
> MENGO
> ¡Mueran tiranos traidores!
> TODOS
> ¡Traidores tiranos mueran!
>
> (1811–14)

6

> TODOS
> ¡Fuente Ovejuna! ¡Viva el rey Fernando!
> ¡Mueran malos cristianos, y traidores!
>
> (1882–83)

7See Larson 95–100

8See Larson 109–12.

9For the chroniclers' accounts, see Rades 79^V–80^R; Palencia 286–87. Since all subsequent citations from these chroniclers will be to the pages indicated, no further page references will be given.

10Palencia: "La única queja del vecindario parecía ser el aumento de pechos por causa de las rentas anuales."

11For what follows, see E. Cabrera et al. 122.

12On Cordoba during this period, see the excellent book by J. Edwards.

13For a more detailed discussion of all this process, see Cabrera et al. 113–17; Ramírez de Arellano 448–50.

[14]See MacKay 131–42

[15]See *Cortes,* 394–401

[16]". . . vuestra sennoria ha dado çiertas aldeas e villas e logares de algunas çibdades e villas e las ha deuidido e apartado dellas para las dar desde diez annos a esta parte, enlo qual las dichas çibdades e villas han rresçebido grant agrauio e danno."

[17]". . . fazer rresistençia actual o verbal de qual quier qualidad que sea o ser pueda, avn que sea con tumulto de gentes de armas e quier se cunpla o non cunpla la tal merçet o donaçion."

[18]". . . los vezinos delas tales çibdades e villas e logares e castillos se puedan tornar e tornen ala vuestra corona rreal de vuestros rregnos por su propia actoridad en qual quier tienpo e rresistyr por fuerça de armas e en otra manera al tal aquien fuere fecha la dicha merçet syn pena alguna."

[19]For what follows, see Cabrera et al. 117–19; Ramírez de Arellano 452–57.

[20]". . . porque vos mando a todos e a cada uno de vos que vos juntades e vades a los dichos logares e sus terminos . . . e los entredes e tomedes e vos apoderedes de ellos . . . para mi e para la mi corona de mis regnos e para esa dicha çibdad de Cordoba."

[21]". . . de se alzar e rebelar para nos e para la nuestra corona real sin por ello caer ni incurrir en pena ni calunia alguna."

[22]"Auia hecho aquel Cauallero maltratamiento a sus vassallos, teniendo en la villa muchos soldados para sustentar en ella la voz del Rey de Portugal, que pretendia ser Rey de Castilla: y consentia que aquella descomedida gente hiziesse grandes agrauios y afrentas a los de Fuenteovejuna, sobre comerseles sus haziendas. Vltra desto, el mesmo Comendador mayor auia hecho grandes agrauios y deshonras a los de la villa, tomandolos por fuerça sus hijas y mugeres, y robandoles sus haziendas, para sustentar aquellos soldados que tenia . . ."

[23]For this new and important evidence, see Cabrera et al. 119. The interdict may also help to explain the absence of one feature, the ringing of bells to summon the populace, which was a traditional constituent element in Castilian urban unrest.

[24]Palencia: "Después se apoderaron del oro, plata y otras riquezas, y se ensañaron con los criados del Comendador, antes sus amigos."

[25]Rades: " . . . determinaron todos de vn consentimiento y voluntad alçarse contra el [*comendador*] y matarle." Palencia refers to "secretas reuniones celebradas en los escondrijos de los montes" and states: "En aquellos escondrijos tenían sus conciliábulos y allí maquinaba la multitud la desgracia del infeliz Comendador."

[26]Palencia: "la inicua conjuración de los de Fuenteovejuna"; Rades: "estauan conjurados."

[27]For an excellent analysis of these traditional forms of organization, see Gutíerrez Nieto 319–67.

[28]Gutíerrez Nieto 338: "Así, en 1296, en el concejo de Cuenca, todos los vecinos se juramentarán de 'ser todos unos' para la conservación de la ciudad en el realengo, defensa de su fuero, que se cumpla el recto ejercicio de la justicia y para que nadie 'no faga tuerto ni fuerza ni deshonra ni soberbia'."

[29]Gutíerrez Nieto 354.

[30]"Fue de la Corte vn Iuez Pesquisidor a Fuenteovejuna, con comision de los Reyes Catholicos, para aueriguar la verdad de este hecho, y castigar a los culpados: y avn que

dio tormento a muchos de los que se avian hallado en la muerte del Comendador mayor, nunca ninguno quiso confessar quales fueron los capitanes o primeros mouedores de aquel delicto, ni dixieron los nombres de los que en el se auian hallado. Preguntauales el Iuez, Quien mato al Comendador mayor? Respondian ellos, Fuenteovejuna. Preguntauales, Quien es Fuenteovejuna? Respondian, Todos los vezinos desta villa. Finalmente todas sus respuestas fueron a este tono, por que estauan conjurados, que avn que los matassen a tormentos no auian de responder otra cosa. Y lo que mas es de admirar, que el Iuez hizo dar tormento a muchas mugeres y mancebos de poca edad, y tuuieron la misma constancia y animo que los varones muy fuertes."

[31]Rades: " . . . se juntaron . . . los Alcaldes, Regidores, Iusticia y Regimiento con los otros vezinos, y con mano armado, entraron por fuerça en las casas de la Encomienda mayor, donde el dicho Comendador estaua."

[32]See Cabrera et al. 119–21.

[33]Palencia: "Mensajeros enviados por D. Rodrigo Girón y D. Alfonso de Aguilar para preparar sus dañados fines, les excitaron a dar muerte al Comendador . . . "

[34]Rades: "Estando en esto, antes que acabasse de espirar, acudieron las mugeres de la villa, con Panderos y Sonages, a regozijar la muerte de su señor: y auian hecho para esto vna Vandera, y nombrado Capitana y Alferez. Tambien los mochachos a imitacion de sus madres hizieron su Capitania, y puestos en la orden que su edad permitia, fueron a solenizar la dicha muerte, tanta era la enemistad que todos tenian contra el Comendador mayor."

[35]See Gutiérrez Nieto 341–42.

[36]For these examples, Gutíerrez Nieto 342, 349–50.

[37]Rades: " . . . la voz del Rey de Portogal, que pretendia ser Rey de Castilla."

[38]Rades: " . . . y alli todos los hombres y mugeres le hizieron pedaços, arrastrandole, y haziendo en el grandes crueldades y escarnios."

[39]See *Poema de mio Cid* 3283–90.

[40]*Siete Partidas,* Part 2, *Tit.* 28, *Ley* 2: " . . . que lo matassen cruelmente por ello, rastrandolo, o desmembrandolo, en manera que todos tomassen escarmiento, para non fazer otro tal"; "la mas estraña muerte que pudiessen."

[41]*Siete Partidas,* Part 2, *Tit.* 28, *Ley* 2: "Ca non lo touo por bien Santa Eglesia, que fuessen soterrados en lugares sagrados. Ante mandaron, que si lo fallaron y metidos, que sacassen ende sus huesos, e los derramassen por los campos, o los quemassen . . ."

[42]*Siete Partidas, Part* 1, *Tit.* 9, *Ley* 15; *Part* 1, *Tit.* 13, *Ley* 8.

[43]"Los de Fuenteovejuna despues de auer muerto al Comendador mayor, quitaron las varas y cargos de justicia a los que estauan puestos por esta Orden, cuya era la jurisdicion: y dieron las a quien quisieron. Luego acudieron a la ciudad de Cordoua, y se encomendaron a ella, diziendo querian ser subjetos a su jurisdicion, como auian sido antes que la villa viniesse a poder de don Pedro Giron."

[44]See Gutiérrez Nieto 356–57; McKendrick 250.

[45]These have been published by Ramírez de Arellano 476–503.

[46]Ramírez de Arellano 492: " . . . comenzó a oir e librar pleitos e dio por su sentencia que todos esten e vivan en paz e concordia . . . "

[47]Ramírez de Arellano 488: " . . . e cada uno dellos en el dicho nombre de los dichos senores concejo de la dicha cibdad pidieron a mi el dicho escribano publico e notario que les diese a cada uno testimonio en publica forma firmado e signado . . . "

[48]Ramírez de Arellano 494: " . . . tomaron por las manos al dicho Pedro Rodriguez Cobo procurador de los dichos senores concejo de la dicha cibdad de Cordoba . . . e metieronle e pusieronle corporalmente de pies dentro de la dicha villa de Fuente Bexuna . . . e el dicho Pedro Rodriguez Cobo . . andovo corporalmente de pies dentro en la dicha villa por la calle que esta delante de la dicha puerta de Sant Sebastian de unas partes a otras e cerro sobre si las puertas de la dicha villa de la dicha portada contra el campo e luego abriolas lo qual . . . dijo . . . . lo habia fecho e facia e fizo en senal de reintegracion e restitucion."

[49]See Ramírez de Arellano 491, 497, 500–01.

[50]Ramírez de Arellano 502: " . . . tomo con sus manos una lanza e derribo e derroco la corteza de la pared de encima de la dicha puerta que dicen de la cal maestra de parte de dentro de la villa que estaban ende pintadas ciertas figuras e armas que diz eran las armas del dicho comendador mayor."

[51]Ramírez de Arellano 492: " . . . subio e se asento en el dicho poio e consistorio e en senal de la dicha posesion . . . e como alcalde mayor de la dicha cibdad de Cordoba e su tierra en presencia de la dicha gente comenzo a oir e librar pleitos e dio por su sentencia que todos esten e vivan en paz e concordia."

[52]Ramírez de Arellano 500: "E luego incontinente en el dicho dia e mes e ano e hora suso dichos en la dicha presencia de nos los dichos Gomez Gonzalez e Gomez Fernandez escribanos publicos e notarios el dicho Juan de Berrio se asento en el dicho poio e consistorio como alcalde mayor para oir e librar pleitos retificando usando e continuando la dicha posesion . . . "

Works Cited

ALFONSO X. *Siete Partidas. Los códigos españoles concordados y anotados.* 12 vols. Madrid: M. Rivadeneyra, 1872–73.

BLUM, JEROME. *The End of the Old Order in Rural Europe.* Princeton: Princeton UP, 1978.

CABRERA, EMILIO, et al. "La sublevación de Fuenteovejuna contemplada en su V centenario." *Actas del I Congreso de Historia de Andalucía: Andalucía Medieval.* Vol. 2. Córdoba: Publicaciones del Monte de Piedad y Caja de Ahorros de Córdoba, 1978. 113–22.

Cortes de los antiguos reinos de León y de Castilla. La Real Academia de la Historia. Vol. 3. Madrid: M. Rivadeneyra, 1866.

DAVIS, NATALIE ZEMON. "The Rites of Violence: Religious Riot in Sixteenth-Century France." *Past and Present* 59 (1973): 59–91.

EDWARDS, JOHN. *Christian Cordoba: The City and Its Region in the Late Middle Ages.* Cambridge: Cambridge UP, 1982.

GUTÍERREZ NIETO, JUAN IGNACIO: "Semántica del término Comunidad antes de 1520: Las asociaciones juramentadas de defensa." *Hispania* 136 (1977): 319–67.

HERRERO, JAVIER. "The New Monarchy: A Structural Reinterpretation of Fuenteovejuna." *Revista Hispánica Moderna* 36 (1970–71): 173–85.

LARSON, DONALD R. *The Honor Plays of Lope de Vega.* Cambridge: Harvard UP, 1977.

MACKAY, ANGUS. *Spain in the Middle Ages: From Frontier to Empire, 1000–1500.* London: Macmillan, 1977.

MCKENDRICK, GERALDINE. "The *Dança de la Muerte* of 1520 and Social Unrest in Seville." *Journal of Hispanic Philology* 3 (1979): 239–59.

PALENCIA, ALONSO DE. *Crónica de Enrique IV.* 3 vols. Ed. A. Paz y Mélia. Madrid: M. Rivadeneyra, 1973–75.

Poema de mio Cid. Ed. Colin Smith. Oxford: Clarendon, 1972.

RADES Y ANDRADA, FRANCISCO DE. *Crónica de las tres órdenes de Santiago, Calatrava y Alcántara.* Ed. D. Lomax. Barcelona: Ediciones El Albir, 1980.

RAMÍREZ DE ARELLANO, RAFAEL. "Rebelíon de Fuente Obejuna contra el comendador mayor de Calatrava Fernán Gómez de Guzmán." *Boletín de la Real Academia de la Historia* 39 (1901): 446–512.

SALOMON, NOËL, *Recherches sur le thème paysan dans la "comedia" au temps de Lope de Vega.* Bordeaux: Bordeaux UP, 1965.

VEGA CARPIO, LOPE DE, and CRISTOBAL DE MONROY. *Fuente Ovejuna (Dos Comedias).* Ed. Francisco López Estrada. Madrid: Castalia, 1969.

A Provincial Masque of
COMUS, 1636

MARTIN BUTLER

O NE OF THE most neglected areas of English theater history is the provincial stage under James I and Charles I. Inevitably, critical attention has tended to focus on the London stages in this period to the exclusion of the less interesting provincial drama; the history of the latter at this time is generally conceded to be one of contraction and decline, in which lies the principal cause of its comparative neglect. Yet the provincial stage survived in attenuated form right down to the outbreak of the Civil War. Despite the greater rewards for theatrical enterprise offered in London, some players clung tenaciously to the old touring tradition, while some towns continued to open their gates to strollers down to 1642, and it can be telling and illuminating to consider the state of theatrical activity at the center in the total context of playing nationwide.[1] Moreover, the early Stuart period saw the rise of one particular kind of provincial theatrical entertainment—the amateur masque or show, mounted at a great house privately or semi-privately within a circle of friends, family, and, possibly neighbors and tenants—which does demand some attention as a form novel in this period and which, perhaps, is especially characteristic of it. I count at least fourteen such shows performed in the provinces under James I and Charles I, and there is circumstantial evidence which would suggest that the total should go yet higher. One of these shows, at least, we would not willingly let die—Milton's *Masque at Ludlow Castle,* which establishes the possibilities of the form at its highest stage of elaboration.

A second reason for the neglect of this subject is the general thinness of the documentation that has survived. Payments made to touring troupes have come down to us, and about some kinds of atypical amateur provincial playing (such as that associated with royal progresses or student productions in the universities) we are relatively well informed. But concerning the amateur masque we are completely in the dark, and there are many questions which it would be helpful to have answered; in particular we need to know more concerning the capabilities and limitations of provincial staging. How elaborate were the provincial masques? What scenery was the artistocratic theater capable of mounting? How expensive was it? Who designed it? Did its technology and taste keep pace with the distant splendors of Whitehall? Answers to such questions would greatly aid our imaginative reconstruction of the circumstances of Milton's *Masque;* they might also tell us something about the sophistication of theatrical activity in the country at large, as opposed to Whitehall about which we know so much already.

Hence the importance of the recovery of an apparently full set of accounts for the performance of a private masque by the Clifford family, earls of Cumberland, at Skipton in or around April 1636. The involvement of the Cliffords in the patronage of provincial playing is already well known. Many payments relevant to theatrical matters (principally payments to troupes of players touring in Yorkshire) were first extracted from the Clifford accounts by T. D. Whitaker for his *History of Craven* (1805), and these, by way of J. T. Murray's *English Dramatic Companies* (1910), found their way into the records of provincial playing listed in the first volume of G. E. Bentley's *The Jacobean and Caroline Stage* (1941). Murray had listed the payments to strollers, rather confusingly, as "Craven district" visits, and under this unhelpful title they reappear in Bentley. In fact they relate to performances at two of the principal Clifford residences, Skipton Castle in the West Riding, and Londesborough in the East Riding of Yorkshire. In 1960 a comprehensive and systematic collection of relevant entries from the accounts was made by Lawrence Stone.[2] By this time some of the payments which Whitaker and Murray had seen were lost and Stone was unable to trace them, but all three historians had overlooked one or two additional items, including the details of preparations for the masque at Skipton in 1636 (I include two other entries omitted by Stone as an appendix to this article).

The necessary and useful context for the accounts of the Skipton masque is a brief summary of the history of the Cliffords and of their situation at the time of the performance. The family was an ancient noble dynasty that possessed extensive tracts of land throughout Yorkshire, Westmorland, and the border and exerted a stranglehold on the Craven district around Skipton.[3] The Cliffords had held a barony since 1299, and the court career of the third Earl of Cumberland, George Clifford (d. 1605), as champion to Queen Elizabeth and as the promoter of a series of famous privateering expeditions, had been especially spectacular. However, under the Stuarts and largely as a result of George Clifford's prodigality, the family finances underwent a sudden and rapid collapse. The fourth earl, Francis Clifford (1559–1641), encumbered with his predecessor's massive debts, improvidently ran down the permanent value of his estates by selling off land and granting long leases to his tenants to meet his immediate cash needs. He was kept solvent by a profitable license to export cloth which he held by grant from the Crown, but this expired in 1626, plunging the family into renewed crisis. Drastic sales of land followed and the remaining estates were systematically racked, but the earl still failed fully to clear off his debts and in the 1630s a shrunken income was forcing household economies onto him. The earl despairingly left affairs in the hands of his son, Henry, Lord Clifford (1591–1643); his niece, Anne Clifford, said that she had heard that "he is sometimes besides his wits, but that his son does what he can to conceal it, lest his father should beggar him" (Williamson 147). Nevertheless the debts remained unpaid and continued to rise sharply. Rents in the East Riding were doubled in 1635, and in the two years before the Skipton masque Henry Clifford had borrowed over £2000 at London. Another crisis was impending. In 1637 the debts stood at £6600 and Henry asked his brother-in-law, the lord deputy of Ireland, to plead with the king to repay money the family had been owed (as was the royal way) for ten years.

Two years later a "benevolence" was forced out of the tenants, but by
1641 the creditors had begun to go to law for recovery of their money,
and the collapse was rendered complete during the short earldom of
Henry Clifford (1641–43) by expenses incurred at the outbreak of the
Civil War. In his will Henry Clifford lamented that "greate debts" inhibited him from giving "my ould and faithfull servants" more than
"sum small legacyes," and "with anguish of soule" he wrote:

I bewaile the miserable condicion of my decayed fortune, which disables me
to give any present supplye to my distressed and dear daughter, the Lady Dun-
garvan, and hir sweete children, whoe from hir infancy hath beene the greatest comfort of my life and ioye of my heart, and nowe is like to be left by me
distressed and afflicted, separated from hir dear and noble husband and his estate. . . . (Clay 398)

At his death the great consolidated estates disintegrated. Some debts
were still unpaid as late as 1665.[4]

The Cliffords were a prime example of the decline of the old aristocracy and of the difficulties they faced in keeping pace with economic
change; yet they compounded their problems by throwing away
much-needed money on extravagances deliberately and conspicuously cultivated in the face of their actual progressive impoverishment.
Sinking to the level of the lesser nobility, Henry Clifford erected a bar-
rier against social and psychological insecurity (such as had afflicted
his father) by living as if he were still a great aristocrat, participating
prominently in the pleasures of court society, patronizing fashionable
artists such as the painter Daniel Mytens and the sculptor Nicholas
Stone, and carefully exhibiting the traditional hospitality appropriate
to a great household (566 meals were served to guests in one week
alone in 1629).[5] A genuine financial purpose was served by such dis-
plays of aristocratic liberality and ostentatious indifference toward
money, for the Cliffords, undergoing attrition at court, needed to
maintain the dignity suitable to their status in order to compete suc-
cessfully for the royal favors and offices which might have alleviated
their problems (and which in fact eluded them), but, ironically, such
strategies themselves contributed to the condition which they were
intended to cure. The family was caught in a financial double bind, a
spiral of unproductive but inflationary expenditure, as was perceived

by the friend of Henry Clifford who advised him in 1622 that "my lorde your father [should] now take occasion to lessen his expenses of housekeeping, whereof (as your l'p knoweth) ther is som need; and that your l'p, in your sportes, wil drawe as lyttle company as you may, wherein you shall both keep decorum, and ease your charges" (Whitaker 366).

However, Henry Clifford was determined to attract company and keep no decorum but the highest, and against this background of financial insecurity and distress, his patronage of provincial playing is extremely revealing. Far from being the casual amusement of an isolated household, players provided the family with yet another means of reinforcing their aristocratic confidence. Remarkably, not only did the Cliffords invite strolling troupes into their homes, but they displayed an interest in all the varieties of theatrical performance which were possible in the provinces. Henry Clifford seems to have organized what we might term command performances of favorite plays in the country, for special arrangements were made for *The Knight of the Burning Pestle* and *A New Way to Pay Old Debts* to be staged at Skipton in 1636, and he certainly held a joint sponsorship in a company of provincial players (even though the patronage of theatrical companies was theoretically in the royal gift alone), for "Georg Corden Servaunt to the Earle of Leic, Willm Johnson servaunt to the lord Clifford Georg Sanderson servant to the Lord Goring & 13 more assistants players" turned up at Coventry and Leicester in the 1630s (Murray 2: 254; cf.319). In 1617 the family had been responsible for a royal welcome, when they entertained King James on his way back from Scotland at Brougham Castle in Westmorland with a show written by Thomas Campion,[6] and we may assume that the similar prodigality involved in staging the later masque at Skipton was, if more limited, still carefully cultivated. The range and variety of the family's theatrical interests are extremely impressive, and doubtless they were designed to reassure the Cliffords of their importance while displaying the solidity of their local base. Around 1630, the prologue for a (lost) private masque staged by the Earl of Middlesex at Wiston in Sussex included a recognition of the extravagance of the occasion in the apologetic lines that "tis for Kings / Not for their subjects, to have such rare things," but the poet, Sir John Suckling, was consoling his patron for the public political disgrace which he had recently sustained (Suckling 1: 28). By contrast, Henry Clifford was using his private theatricals vigorously to assert his ability still to compete, and it is likely that the Skipton masque would have addressed itself to proclaiming loudly the family's hold on that dynastic prestige which was, in actual fact, slipping inexorably through their grasp.

The Clifford papers are a vast and complex series of documents, estates records, and account books now deposited in the library at Chatsworth. The masque accounts occupy the greater part of two and a half leaves (fols. 181–83) of Bolton MS. 175 at Chatsworth. This volume is a book of receipts and disbursements made in 1636 by Robert Robotham, secretary and purse-bearer to Francis, and, later, Henry Clifford. The accounts are headed "1636 Extraordinaryes &c," and they occur at the end of the volume, following several blank pages, which is doubtless why Lawrence Stone missed them in 1960. However, when Stone perused the accounts, the "extraordinary" payments had already been seen by Walter L. Woodfill, who selected twenty items for an appendix to his *Musicians in English Society from Elizabeth to Charles I* (1953). I have reexamined the volume at Chatsworth and I reproduce the complete set of accounts for the masque here for the first time. I have omitted only the half-dozen or so "extraordinary" items which have no connection with the masque (except the first payment included here, which may or may not belong with the masque), and Robotham's subtotaling of the payments at the foot of each page. For the sake of clarity I have expanded contractions and regularized the lineation of the accounts. Interlineations are placed between the symbols ⌐ ¬ .

[Chatsworth, Bolton MS. 175]
[fol. 181ʳ]

	For mending the drum—	0–1–0
	For flax & pastboard—	0–1–0
first maske	To Paule for going to Yorke	0–4–6
	for thinges for the maske	
	For 6 pre of gloues for the maskers—	0–8–0
	For 3 dozen of ribbining of one sort—	0–9–0
	For 29 yardes of another—	0–14–6
	For tape, nayles &c	[ ]
	For .6. paire of pumps in part .3ˢ —	0–3: 0

[fol. 181ᵛ]

For the mask	For 3 sheetes of pastboard—	0: 0: 9
	For Tinfoyle & diuerse	
	cullers for Henrick—	00:12: 7
	For Torches & Wax candles—	00:10: 6
	For horne flowres—	00:07: 0
	For 6oz purle—	00:07: 0
	For Assindew & bells—	00: 4: 0
	For Oes spangles & gloues—	00: 2: 4
	For 12. sheetes of pastboard—	00: 3: 0
	For more Assindew—	00: 2: 0
	For Paules jorney to Yorke wᵗʰ horses	
	for the Musick of the Citty—	00:10: 0
	For 6 sheets of lattin—	00–2–6
	To Hugh Barrons & Moreby for bringing	
	thinges to Skipton from Yorke	00: 2: 6
	For their suppers—	00: 1: 0
	My Charges in going to Yorke to buy	
	the propertyes following & these	
	thinges abousaid being abroad .3.	00: 9: 6
	nightes my selfe & horse	
	For sending a messinger to Yorke—	00: 4:00
	For browne paper for the	
	plaisterer and for thrid—	00:01–00
	For stockinges for mocion [sic]—	00:02: 6
	For .4. branch Candlesticks making—	00:05: 6
	For 8 dayes worke of a joyner—	00:05: 6
	For lattin for the Candlesticks—	00:04: 0
	For a yard of Callicoe—	00: 2: 0

[fol. 182ʳ]

Adhuc yᵉ Mask	For 7 pairs of pumpes & shoes	
	for the maskers—	00:12: 0
	To Tho: Bleasdell for tayler worke	00: 8: 0
	for Comus & his Companye—	
	To Tho. Moreby for the hyer of 4 horses	
	wᶜʰ the waytes of Yorke to Yorke [sic]—	1:00:00
	To the waytes of Yorke ⌐for their Attendance	
	at Mask⌐ —	5–00–0
	To John Gerdler ⌐for himselfe⌐ —	1–00–0
	To Adam Gerdler—	1–00–0
	To the boyes—	0–10–0
	To the boy wᶜʰ daunced—	0–2–0
	To Moreby for charge of the horses—	0–6–0

paid for Ale at Ni Blakays wch they dranck when they toke horse	0–2–6
To Arthur & Harry wch came from Yorke ⌐for their reward⌐ —	2–0–0
To Beniamyne for 3 pare of Buskins for Mr.Earsden, Raph & Cumins & for pumps for others—	1: 3: 6
To Monsr Munjoy for his reward three pounds—	3:00:00
To Mr Henrick de Kesar for part of his charge & reward in working the scene of the maske 3^{li}—	3:00:00

[fol. 182^v]

To the glouer for a paire of gloues for Genius loci—	00: 3: 6
To Bessy Kitchin on Acc:^t of diuerse yardes of Canvas for the scene & diuerse thinges at Maske the somme of forty shillinges—	2:00:00
To Bowcock for a paire of shoes for Genius loci—	00: 2:00
To Mr Calvert of Yorke vpon Acc:^t of .11. yardes of gold tinsell fitting for Skarfes for Comus & his Company the somme of Twenty shillinges—	1:00:00
To Mr Ousman for the charges of Mr Montioyes horse whilest he stayd for him at Yorke—	00:06:00

bill—

To Mr Croftes of Yorke for diuerse thinges bought for the maske as Taffety ribbon buckerams callicoes &c as by the byll appeares the somme of seaven poundes fyue shill—	7: 5:00
To Arthur the joyner for making the ⌐pullyes for the⌐ Candlesticks, & taking downe the scene .5^s —	00: 5:00

[fol. 183^r]

To Montgomery wyfe for gloues ribbon & other things for the first maske 24^s 6^d—	1: 4: 6

The type of festival which these accounts imply was quite remarkable, for it had more in common with the princely magnificences of Whitehall than with the country pastimes of a Yorkshire market town. Skipton, as some payments indicate, was within a day's ride of York, but set among the high Pennines it was far removed from the center of early Stuart England. This was remote and difficult country which would later prove hospitable to heresy; the Cliffords were northern barons of the old sort on whom the crown still relied to police its outlying parts. The cost of the event was minimal by royal standards (the payments total £38 10s 2d) but in local terms it must have been a notable celebration, its preparation necessitating, as the accounts suggest, an extensive period of busy, intensive work for the whole Clifford household. Arthur the joiner took eight days to construct the scenery and was paid afterward for dismantling it all again. Robotham himself spent three days in York buying properties, and over £5 was expended on carriage alone as persons and materials trundled to and fro between York and Skipton. Moreover the occasion must have been notable for emulating, however distantly, the elaborate and cultivated splendors of the Stuart masque. The Cliffords arranged for music, a scene, and richly dressed masquers, and the payments for the named characters "Genius loci" and "Comus & his Company" can probably be taken to imply that the entertainment involved at least some kind of acted fable or antimasque. There seem to have been seven main masquers dancing at Skipton, for the accounts mention six pairs of gloves and a part payment for six pairs of pumps; then another pair of gloves is added, and when the pumps are paid off (fol. 182^r) they have increased to seven pairs. It is not clear, though, whether the masquers were identical with "Comus & his Company" or whether we have here two separate groups of performers, masquers and antimasquers.[7] Evidently, too, the Cliffords swelled their local resources with the services of outsiders who could provide special theatrical skills for which there was no normal everyday need at Skipton, and this information is of great interest for our understanding of the conditions of performance that would have applied to Milton's Ludlow masque and to other contemporary amateur entertainments.

Much the largest group of payments went to costume the masquers, nearly £15 being disbursed to find them sufficiently magnificent garb. Costuming was always an expensive item in the court masques. The king's suit for Thomas Carew's *Coelum Britannicum* (1634) cost him in excess of £120, and a page's costume in the same show cost over £20. Such clothes would not be discarded but would be kept in the hope that they might later be reused; the Egerton boys who danced as pages in *Coelum Britannicum* stored their "Maskin cloathes" in a hamper at home and probably wore them a second time in 1634 when they acted at Ludlow.[8] Henry Lord Clifford had a £150 suit which doubtless would have been paraded on this occasion,[9] and the masquers must also have been sumptuously dressed. Taffety was an expensive glossy silk and callicoe an imported Indian cloth; more telling is the quantity of ribboning and ornamental stuff which the Cliffords bought. Oes and spangles (fol. 181[V]) commonly decorated masquing suits at court, where they would actually have been made from precious metals; "purl," six ounces of which were used at Skipton, was a thread or cord made of twisted gold or silver wire, small loops (purls) of which would have been embroidered onto the borders of the suits. The "assindew" of which two purchases were made was a cheap tinsel substitute, a thin brass metal of a bright gold color sometimes used in place of gold leaf and known further south as "arsedine." Tinsel was often employed by court scene painters to highlight the set, as in *Salmacida Spolia* (1640), but it could be used for costumes, too (the king wore tinsel in *Coelum Britannicum,* and a character in an amateur play performed in Northamptonshire in 1640 was dressed *"All in Silver Tinsell"*).[10] Assindew was commonly worn by mummers in West Yorkshire at Christmas,[11] and would have decked the masquers at Skipton; Comus's company sported extremely expensive gold tinsel scarves. It is probably worth noticing that at Ludlow Comus and his rout appeared with their apparel "glistringe" (Milton 59). The Skipton masquers must all have glittered impressively in the candlelight of the hall, and it appears that some or all of them wore ornamental bells (fol. 181[V]). Perhaps the mysterious "horne flowres" should also be counted with the clothing payments. I cannot make much sense of this item, but there are possibly parallel payments in Tudor and Stuart revels accounts for spangled flowers or flowers made from silk and gold for court costumes.[12] Whatever they were, they were a fairly expensive item.

There is every indication that musically the masque was highly competent. The city waits came from York to sing and presumably to provide instrumental music, too. However, as a family the Cliffords were notable for their discriminating musical tastes and patronage, and it may be that some of the music was home produce (the Clifford accounts are full of payments for music of various kinds; the fourth earl was described as one of the "worthy louers and Patrons of that facul-tie" by William Byrd in 1611, and he and his son sponsored Thomas Campion).[13] The solo boy dancer probably belonged to the waits, and Adam and John Gerdler, to whom special gratuities were given, are certainly known to have belonged to the waits as well. These pay-ments indicate that the Gerdlers took prominent roles in the masque, but we do not have to suppose that these were merely singing parts. Adam Gerdler had already appeared in the Clifford records earlier in 1636 when Robotham recorded giving 5s to "Adam Gerdler whome my lord sent for from Yorke to act a part in the Kt of the burning pes-tell," an entry noticed by Murray which has put Gerdler into Bentley's actor-lists as an unknown provincial player (Stone 26). He can now be identified for the first time as a member of the York waits, and his em-ployment by the Cliffords on this second occasion would tend to sug-gest that in April he was acting rather than singing at Skipton. (In pass-ing, his participation in *The Knight of the Burning Pestle* might be taken to suggest that this was not a professional production but an-other amateur affair among the Clifford family.) It is tempting to as-sume that Adam and John Gerdler, the two specifically rewarded per-formers, played the parts of the only two named characters, Comus and the Genius Loci, and possibly in this respect the Cliffords were ex-actly imitating the conventions of the Whitehall masques, in which the speaking parts were taken by professionals while the gentlemanly amateurs confined themselves to the dancing.

The third major item was the scenery, which cost the family over £7 and Arthur eight days' labor. These are the most interesting payments in the accounts, and I discuss them further below. At this stage, we need only note that although this pasteboard and canvas set was far re-moved from Inigo Jones's elaborately carpentered designs it nonethe-less must have been a structure of substance, resplendent in its tinfoil and lattin (a thin, brasslike metal) which were no doubt intended to multiply the beams of the candles, as was the case at court. There is even a hint of special lighting effects in the "pullyes" for the candle-sticks, which might have been winched up to the ceiling, or had mov-able canisters hung over them to darken and lighten them at will, as the Continental scene designers recommended.[14] Henry Clifford fre-quently visited court and would have known well what the production of a masque entailed, and the accounts suggest that however remote from the main currents of Stuart society Skipton may have been, an amateur show could still be staged there in a manner that was highly elaborate and ambitious. Though no text has survived, the accounts demonstrate vividly the resources on which provincial entertainments for which we have no supporting documents might equally well have drawn. The same possibilities of staging, costume, and music which were used at Skipton in 1636 would most likely have been available to Milton and Henry Lawes at Ludlow eighteen months earlier.

What, then, was the text which was performed at Skipton? There are, of course, two famous masques which boast a character called Comus, and it is necessary to consider each briefly here, though neither fits the details of the accounts especially well. Jonson's *Pleasure Reconciled to Virtue,* performed at court in 1618, opened with the entry of Comus, as god of the belly, and his defeat by the athletic Hercules. There is little here to correspond with the expenditures in the Clifford papers, except that Jonson used an unusually large proportion of song, and an antimasque of pigmies that might be echoed in the "boy wch danced" at Skipton. This masque was not yet in print, but there is a contemporary manuscript copy by Ralph Crane, scrivener to the King's Players. This, as it happens, is also in the library at Chatsworth, but it arrived there by a different route from the Clifford accounts, having been in the Cavendish library at Hardwick in 1872, and their present common location is no more than a coincidence.[15] It may be worth remarking that *Pleasure Reconciled to Virtue* would have been an appropriate choice for repetition at Skipton since scenically it is one of the least demanding court masques; but had the Cliffords gone so far as to restage privately in the countryside a masque originally designed for a royal audience it would have been a unique and quite extraordinary occasion indeed.

The other possibility is Milton's *Mask at Ludlow,* which was written specifically for provincial performance. This, too, was unpublished in 1636, but Henry Lawes's preface to the 1637 edition indicates that it was already circulating extensively in manuscript copies. The potential parallels here are more plausible: the country dances of *Comus* would be better suited to Skipton than the subtle choreography of *Pleasure Reconciled to Virtue;* the Genius Loci might have been Robotham's periphrasis for Milton's "guardian spirit," while the "browne paper for the plaisterer" might well have gone to make animal heads for Comus's crew. However the waits and seven masquers would have had little to do in *Comus* and, crucially, the Cliffords could not have reproduced Milton's functional casting. *Comus* was carefully tailored to the requirements of parents who wished to see their teenage daughter and two young sons acting, but Henry Clifford had only one daughter, and she had been recently married. *Comus* is so critically dependent on the ages and identities of the Egerton children who acted in it that it is difficult to see how it could have been remounted at Skipton without substantial alteration. Yet the comparison is not a complete dead-end for the Skipton masque presents a telling parallel case for the kinds of constraints and requirements Milton must have been under when writing *his* provincial entertainment, as well as providing an example of accounts of the type of which must once have existed for Comus, although they have since vanished. Moreover, the reappearance of a Comus character so soon after Milton's masque confirms Henry Lawes's statement in the preface to Milton's published text that the *Mask at Ludlow* had indeed generated significant interest beyond the immediate circle of the Egertons and their acquaintances. Henry Clifford may not have been restaging the *Mask at Ludlow* at Skipton, but the reappearance of a Comus character in his entertainment need not be so simple as a mere case of coincidence.

So we seem to be dealing with a lost text and have no clues concerning its authorship. The "Monsr Munjoy" or "Montioye" who received a large sum in the accounts must have had a significant function in preparing the event, but I doubt that he was the poet. I have been completely unable to trace him anywhere else, and my guess is that he was involved in arranging the dances. Many seventeenth-century dancing masters were expatriate Frenchmen, so much so that this type was satirized on stage in the 1630s and 1650s.[16] This would have given him a sufficiently important role to warrant his reward. The one poet from whom the family is known to have commissioned an entertainment, Campion, was dead, but the Cliffords were well connected and could easily have been put in touch with a budding amateur, like Milton, or a minor professional dramatist such as Thomas Nabbes whose *The Spring's Glory*, published in 1638 with no indication of where it was performed, seems to belong more to the world of amateur country theatricals than to the London theaters.[17] A member of the family might even have written it, rather as Sir John Salusbury and Mildmay Fane, Earl of Westmorland, each produced his own plays in the provinces in the 1640s. Henry Clifford was himself an occasional versifier who had written "poetical translations" of the Song of Solomon and of some Psalms, and his keen interest in the Whitehall entertainments is suggested by the purchases of "two masque books" in 1633 and another "masque book" in 1635 (Aurelian Townshend's two court masques were published in 1632, and Carew's *Coelum Britannicum* in 1634) (Wood 3: 82–83; Woodfill 259). Maybe he would have set his hand to writing speeches and songs for the family.

Probably we should imagine the performance as consisting of (say) an action, played by outsiders and complimentary to the Cliffords, involving Genius Loci and Comus, god of pleasure and his crew, followed by a grand entry of seven masquers drawn from the household or from friends; or possibly the masquers themselves posed as sons of Comus, followers of pleasure. These were the usual, appropriate characters found frequently in local shows. For example, a genius of the place appeared in Jonson's Theobald's entertainment (1607), Milton's *Arcades,* and Sir John Salusbury's Chirk Castle masque (1634). The Penates or household gods took part in Jonson's Highgate welcome (1604), Silvanus god of the woods in Campion's Caversham entertainment (1613), the buttery spirit in the anonymous Coleoverton masque (1618), and the Lars Familiaris in Cockayne's *Masque at Bretby* (1640). Milton's Sabrina is another such figure connected with local myth and legend. It is likely, too, that the Skipton entertainment was in two or more sections, since it would have been punctuated by the action(s) implied by the payment to Hendrik de Keyser for "working the scene of the maske" (fol. 182^r). This is the most remarkable entry in the whole accounts and needs to be considered in detail. It suggests strongly not only that even this remote provincial performance had a scenic set but that the scenery was *changeable,* that even in what must have been technically the most difficult department the Cliffords were capable of reproducing in minature the coveted effects of the court masque.

The scenic resources of the amateur stages down to the Civil War were limited but not inadequate. A surprisingly high proportion of country productions called for flying effects, and several involved moving or changing scenery. Milton's *Comus,* with three changes of scene, was an unusually elaborate production, equaled only by the anonymous *King and Queen's Entertainment at Richmond* (1636) which was, of course, a state occasion. More commonplace were the discoveries of scenes or masquers, either by the drawing of a curtain (or two) or by the opening of a scenic structure, such as a bower or temple. Insofar as we can build on Robotham's casual phraseology, the Skipton set was more elaborate than this: the "scene of the maske" sounds like a more substantial structure than an opening bower, and "working the scene" like a more complicated operation than merely drawing a traverse or sliding back a door. But the special interest of these accounts lies in their mention of the name of the architect of the masque, the only such identification, as far as I am aware, that we have for the provincial drama. Hendrik de Keyser offers us for the first time the opportunity of exploring in an informed way some of the procedures by which a country family might have set about seeking to stage such an entertainment. Moreover, the connection which his name provides with the contemporary theater in Holland throws a startling and suggestive sidelight on the development of scenic staging at this time in England at large.

Hendrik de Keyser (1613–65), the youngest son of an Amsterdam city architect also named Hendrik, was one of a large number of Low Countries artists working in England in the seventeenth century. The ties across the Channel were strong for religious reasons, and many of these men (though not specifically de Keyser) were Protestant refugees. Alien craftsmen exerted an important influence on the development of English arts and manufactures, contributing especially to the cloth industry and to the subsidiary metal trades, such as copper-beating, brass-making, wire-drawing, pin manufacture, and armaments. The impact of Dutch artists on English painting is well established; less well-known is the colony of Dutch and French sculptors resident in London, centering on a group of leading names or families—the Colts, Jansens, Cures, and Christmases, and Hubert le Sueur. This is a circle with which de Keyser would have been familiar.[18]

Hendrik's father (1565–1621) was the most important native sculptor working in the north of Holland at the beginning of the seventeenth century. The creator of Dutch neoclassicism, he was responsible for several notable buildings in Amsterdam, including two churches and the Amsterdam Exchange, modeled on Gresham's Royal Exchange which in 1606 he came to England to inspect. He also sculpted the effigy on the tomb of William the Silent, and, as we shall see, had connections with the theater. His sons carried on his work as, variously, stonemasons, architects, and popular portrait painters; Willem de Keyser would hold his father's post as Master Mason to the city of Amsterdam. More significantly, the English sculptor Nicholas Stone met de Keyser in London in 1606 and followed him back to Amsterdam to train in his studio, eventually marrying one of his daughters. Stone returned to England in 1613 to set up his own studio, but the connection remained important. In 1634 he was joined by Willem and Hendrik the younger.[19]

Hendrik II remained in England until Stone's death in 1647. Little is known of his work; in later life he became a member of the mason's guild at Amsterdam and worked on the design of municipal buildings there.[20] In England he was probably occupied in much the same manner as other alien craftsmen, producing a range of small commissions for minor gentry, such as tombs, fireplaces, doors, and occasionally more substantial projects depending on the fluctuating demand for his specialist skills. Useful comparisons, if a little too elevated, are the careers of the de Caus architects, Salomon de Caus (d. 1626) and his son, or nephew, Isaac (d. 1656). This family were French Protestants, and Salomon de Caus worked in the household of Prince Henry, tutoring him in mathematics and building galleries and fountains at Richmond. After Henry's death he followed Princess Elizabeth to Heidelberg, where he laid out the castle gardens and wrote treatises on mechanics and hydraulics. Isaac remained in England working on royal projects, including the grotto beneath Inigo Jones's Banqueting House, but in the 1630s he was employed by various aristocratic families, acting as the executant architect for the Earl of Bedford at Woburn and Covent Garden, and working for the Earl of Pembroke at Wilton and for the Earl of Cork.[21] Other Low Countries craftsmen moved permanently into the provinces: Theodoricus de Have worked at Cambridge and King's Lynn in the 1560s, Bernard Dininghoff produced stained glass and gatehouses in Yorkshire in the 1580s, Joseph Hollemans sculpted monuments in Warwickshire and Northamptonshire in the 1590s, David Papillon designed military fortifications for Parliament in the Civil War.[22] Their activities indicate the range and variety of skills the seventeenth-century architect was expected to be able to provide, and it is work such as this that we should imagine Hendrik de Keyser doing, probably for a number of northern families, in the 1630s. In Nicholas Stone's correspondence for 1639 he is mentioned in passing as traveling to Hull, and described as "brother Hendrik in the country." He was almost certainly the same man as "Henrik, the Dutch engineer" who was employed in the king's army during the Bishops' War of 1639 to strengthen the defenses at Hull, and then "sent back to finish the works at Carlisle" on which he had previously been engaged (Spiers 116–17; Calendar 415).

Probably de Keyser's introduction to the Cliffords came through Stone, who had sculpted a monument for them in Londesborough church, and the Cliffords may well have asked him to contribute to their masque in addition to whatever other projects he was also producing for them at the time, exploiting his mechanical and architectural skills exactly as James and Charles (to compare small things with great) depended on Inigo Jones's technological knowledge to construct the machines they needed for their stages. Thus de Keyser provides us with a backstage view into the pragmatics of mounting a masque, suggesting something of the way in which the various talents necessary for such an entertainment could have been assembled in a relatively remote place. But his particular importance is the interesting link which he offers with Holland, and the informed guess that this enables us to make about the means by which he might have gone about fulfilling his commission, and about the kind of stage design which would have been possible in the provinces.

It is reasonable to suppose that at Skipton de Keyser would have drawn on his past experience of stage production, especially at home in Amsterdam, in the literary and theatrical milieu in which his father had been involved. The theater in Amsterdam was in the hands of the literary guilds, the "chambers of rhetoric," who staged productions on civic occasions and in the Nederduytsche Academie. Hendrik I was a member of the "White Lavender" chamber, and had built the stage for a play to welcome James's daughter Elizabeth and her husband the Palsgrave to Amsterdam in 1613, the year of Hendrik II's birth.[23] This would have been a shallow outdoor stage with a large and elaborately decorated compartmented façade behind, a familiar, traditional design which was the norm for such public occasions. But Hendrik II would also have had experience with changeable scenery for it happens that the Nederduytsche Academie, built in 1617 and after 1632 the only playhouse operating regularly in Amsterdam, was singular for possessing rudimentary machinery for the effecting of scene changes. An inventory of 1622 shows the Academie stage to have boasted "turning cloths" (*omdraeyende doecken*), which Professor W.M.H. Hummelen has shown to have been reversible flats which were painted on both sides, so that when they were turned round mechanically the scenic background of the stage was changed, usually from an interior to an exterior setting, or vice versa, an arrangement that seems to have been unique to this theater.[24] The function of these turning cloths, placed at the rear of the stage in a large central compartment which could be curtained off and used for tableaux and discoveries, was more to decorate the stage appropriately than to create a very strong illusion of scenic verisimilitude as was the case in the Stuart court masques, yet their superiority to the limited scenic devices that were available in the Stuart professional playhouses is clearly marked. It is easy to see how such a principle could be conveniently adapted by a resourceful Dutch architect seeking to provide a cheap and uncomplicated changeable scenic arrangement suitable for a great house situated in a small English provincial town.

De Keyser's background knowledge is suggestive in the context of the Clifford masque and indicates one way in which a piece of theater like this could have been organized. However, the particular reason for bringing this information forward here is its similarity with a fascinating parallel case which has been known about for a long time, yet which has always seemed rather isolated and peripheral to the history of scenic staging in England when considered on its own, but which looks rather more significant when set beside the Skipton masque. In the early 1640s, Mildmay Fane, the second Earl of Westmorland, wrote a series of plays which were staged on his Northamptonshire estate at Apthorpe with discoveries and changeable scenery. Fane has left us a rough sketch, now in the Huntington Library, for a fully changeable set for his play *Candy Restored,* performed at Apthorpe in the spring of 1641.[25] The sketch shows a stage with three pairs of flats at the sides and a rear curtain, each flat being pivoted in the center so it could turn through 180°. An additional diagram indicates how the flats were turned by means of ropes or wires passing under the stage and attached to small arms on the pivots. Fane's play-text specifies that the flats were painted with "*Heroes, men of armes in armes and Battles*" on one side and a peaceful country scene on the other. At a crucial point in the action, which concerns the chasing of discord from a disturbed England, the flats presenting the horrid battles "without a *miletary word turne silently faces about . . . and ar backt wth nothing but fresh greenes & faire garden Landskips*" (Fane 101). The principle of the device is that of Inigo Jones's *periaktoi,* or turning machines, but unlike the *periaktoi* used at court and described in the architectural handbooks, Fane's turning machinery was built not as three-dimensional structures but as two-sided flats. Allardyce Nicoll could find no precedent for Fane's machine except in a French treatise by Jean Dubreuil, *Perspective Pratique* (1642), which explained how scenes might "be made to change further by the use of simple frames. In the middle of the frames are put axles or simply two points of iron that rest in pivots—so that when one turns the frames thus mounted they show first one face and then another" (Nicoll 658). But in 1641 Fane patently could not yet have read Dubreuil, and the obvious, tantalizing significance of de Keyser's employment as a scene designer is the hint it offers of a bridge between this otherwise unprecedented scenic device used in 1641 in Northamptonshire and the established scenic practice of the Amsterdam playhouse in the 1620s and 1630s. It is quite plausible that Fane could have witnessed or heard of a provincial performance in which such a machine was used, or that, as the Cliffords had done, he might have employed as designer a journeyman-architect like de Keyser or possibly even the man himself. Fane's sketches prove nothing about the mounting of the Skipton entertainment, but they do demonstrate how problems of staging with limited resources might be approached in the provinces and the solution which they propose is one that de Keyser would actually have seen used in Amsterdam. It is at least possible that de Keyser's changing scenery would have operated along comparable lines and that he was responsible for introducing into England a system of simple stage ma-

chinery of which Mildmay Fane's sketch is the only authenticated
English example.

I have no wish to place undue stress on something which, in the absence of text or designs, must necessarily remain speculative. But con-
sideration of the circumstances of the staging of the Skipton masque
and of the parallel case at Apthorpe does provoke two corollaries concerning the development of scenic staging in England (which are more
in the way of caveats than conclusions). Firstly, the naturalization of
changeable scenery in England is understood to have been achieved
principally through the work of Inigo Jones for the court masques of
James and Charles, and this means, essentially, that it grew from staging practices that were Italianate, courtly, and spectacular, for Jones's
mind was steeped in the forms and language of the festivals of Medici
despotism. But the involvement of de Keyser, however marginally,
does indicate that other traditions and models were available, too, in
this case scenic practices from northern Europe which were more emblematic than illusionist, and which were not the outgrowth of courtly festivals and state occasions but which had been produced from the
experience of regular performances in the professional playhouses.[26]
(This point carries political as well as artistic weight—*Comus* and
Candy Restored both use the masque form to sabotage and subvert the
assumptions of political elitism which Charles's absolutist stage, with
its perspective scenery and hierarchically ordered spectacle, was designed to reinforce.)

Secondly, the provincial stages provided a space for scenic experimentation, and in this respect they must have been extremely important, more important than is suggested by the rather second-rate literary texts that have survived. The court stage aspired to be
overwhelming and magnificent; it expressed the regality of the king;
its audience was a tiny political elite; and it was horrendously expensive. The professional theaters could not compete on this level; neither was it appropriate for them to do so. Illusionist scenery had no
place in the open-air popular playhouses, and was too large and too
complex to be incorporated easily into the restricted stage areas that
were available in the indoor "private" theaters. The only stages on
which scenic experimentation was possible outside the prestigious
world of the court were, precisely, the amateur stages in the prov-

inces, and it is a particular, recurrent feature of amateur theatricals throughout this period that they involve a continual exploration and elaboration of rudimentary devices of scenery and staging (and this holds good for the amateur stage in London too).[27] This was a function which could not be performed by the professional playhouses and for which the court stage presented perhaps too grand a model, but the very grandeur of the latter may have obscured the minor yet real part played by the amateur provincial stage in helping to establish and naturalize theatrical practices which only became regular features of professional performances after the Restoration. We have tended to think of changeable scenery as essentially a child of the court theater, but in a fully national perspective it is possible to see that there were other contributors to its parentage beside Whitehall.

Appendix

Further payments from the Clifford papers overlooked by Stone

[Bolton MS. 172]
[fol. 77^r]

4 Ja: 1634	This day given to Certeyne men wch came to Act a playe & did before their lo^{ps} the some of—	00:13: 4

[fol. 77^v]

17 Jan	This day giuen to certeyne players Itinerants wch acted before their Lor^{pp}, I say given them for their reward twenty shillings—	1:00:00

Notes

Contributions of various kinds have been made to this essay by Kate Harris, Richard Luckett, Mrs. D. M. Owen, Professor W.M.H. Hummelen, and Professor Walter L. Woodfill. I am grateful to the Duke of Devonshire's librarian, Mr. Michael Pearman, for permission to quote from the Bolton manuscripts, and to Dr. R. T. Spence for permission to make citations from his thesis on the Cliffords.

[1]The outstanding pioneering essay here is by Salingar, Harrison, and Cochrane.

[2]See Stone.

[3]My account of the Cliffords' finances is based principally on Spence. There is a short summary by Batho 282–83. See also Whitaker 311–95.

[4]See Spence 326–31.

[5]See Spence 320n.

[6]See Spink 57–74.

[7]I have assumed throughout that the accounts refer to a single occasion. Although they contain much repetition there is little actual duplication of resources such as we might expect had several entertainments been conflated into one account. The term "first maske" (fol. 181^{r}) should probably be taken to mean "antimasque" or perhaps to refer to some introductory presentation such as (to speculate) a speech of welcome by the "Genius Loci" of the type that can be found in several comparable entertainments. In any case, there is no mention of any "second mask."

[8]See Orgel and Strong 2:568–70; Demaray 101.

[9]See Whitaker 360.

[10]See Orgel and Strong 2:751, 568; Fane 65.

[11]See Wright 1:83.

[12]See Orgel and Strong 2:568–69; Feuillerat 105.

[13]See Stone 18–19; Woodfill 256–60; Spink passim.

[14]See Hewitt 112.

[15]See Historical Manuscripts Commission, *Report* 3:43.

[16]In William Cavendish's *The Variety* (c. 1639–41) and Francis Kirkman's *The Wits* (published 1662).

[17]Although it differs from other country shows in lacking provision for a revels in which the actors could have taken out the spectators to dance.

[18]See Esdaile, "Refugee Sculptors" 254–62.

[19]See Neurdenberg; Rosenberg, Slive, and Hendrik Ter Kuile 229–31, 225–58, 182–83; Whinney 24, 29, 240; Spiers 31–33.

[20]See Neurdenburg 9.

[21]See Colvin, 256–57.

[22]See Esdaile, "Interaction" 80–88; Girouard 26–35.

[23]See Worp 15–16, 23n.

[24]See Hummelen, *Third Globe* 164–89; *Amsterdams* 301–07.

[25]It is reproduced in Fane 135–36, and in Nicoll 658.

[26]The same criteria apply to the illustration of "A Stage-Play" in Jan Comenius's *Orbis Sensualium Pictus* (1656; first English ed. 1659), to which Nicoll compares the disposition of the wings in Fane's design, for this schoolbook published at Nuremberg had its greatest vogue in the Protestant and northern states of Europe (including England).

[27]Scenery was provided at the private performance of Henry Killigrew's *The Conspiracy* (1635) at York House, sponsored by the Earl of Pembroke, which, as far as we can tell, seems to have been emblematic rather than illusionist. N.B. also the scenes at the

Whitehall production of William Habington's *The Queen of Aragon* (1640), an amateur production by members of Pembroke's household.

Works Cited

BATHO, GORDON. *The Agrarian History of England and Wales.* Ed. Joan Thirsk. Cambridge: Cambridge UP, 1967.

Calendar of State Papers. Domestic Series 1639.

CLAY, J. W. "The Clifford Family." *Yorkshire Archaeological Journal* 18 (1905): 354–411.

COLVIN, HOWARD MONTAGU. *A Biographical Dictionary of British Architects 1600–1840.* London: John Murray, 1978.

DEMARAY, JOHN G. *Milton and the Masque Tradition.* Cambridge, Mass.: Harvard UP, 1968.

ESDAILE, K. A. "The Interaction of English and Low Country Sculpture in the Sixteenth Century." *Journal of the Warburg and Courtauld Institute* 6 (1943): 80–88.

_____. "The Part Played by Refugee Sculptors, 1600 to 1750." *Proceedings of the Huguenot Society of London* 18 (1947–52): 254–62.

FANE, MILDMAY. *Raguaillo d'Oceano and Candy Restored.* Ed. Clifford Leech. Louvain: Materials for the Study of the Old English Drama, 1938.

FEUILLERAT, ALBERT GABRIEL. *Documents Relating to the Revels at Court in the Times of King Edward VI and Queen Mary.* Louvain: Materials for the Study of the Old English Drama, 1914.

GIROUARD, MARK. "Some Alien Craftsmen in Sixteenth and Seventeenth-Century England." *Proceedings of the Huguenot Society of London* 20 (1958–64): 26–35.

HEWITT, BARNARD WOLCOTT, *The Renaissance Stage.* Coral Gables: U of Miami P, 1958.

HUMMELEN, WILLEM MARINUS HENDRIK. "Types and Methods of the Dutch Rhetoricians' Theatre." *The Third Globe.* Ed. C. Walter Hodges, Samuel Schoenbaum, and L. Leone. Detroit: Wayne State UP, 1981.

_____. *Amsterdams toneel in het begin van de Gouden Eeuw.* The Hague: Nijhoff, 1982.

MILTON, JOHN. *A Maske: The Earlier Versions.* Ed. Samuel Ernest Sprott. Toronto: U of Toronto P, 1973.

MURRAY, JOHN TUCKER. *English Dramatic Companies 1558–1642.* London: Constable, 1910.

NEURDENBERG, ELIZABETH. *Hendrik de Keyser.* Amsterdam, 1930.

NICOLL, ALLARDYCE. "Scenery between Shakespeare and Dryden." TLS (1936).

ORGEL, STEPHEN, and ROY STRONG. *Inigo Jones: The Theatre of the Stuart Court.* London: Sotheby Parke Bernet, 1973.

ROSENBERG, JAKOB, SEYMOUR SLIVE, and ENGELBERT HENDRIK TER KUILE. *Dutch Art and Architecture.* Harmondsworth: Penguin, 1966.

SALINGAR, LEO, GERALD HARRISON, and BRUCE COCHRANE. "Les comediens et leur public en Angleterre de 1520 à 1640." *Dramaturgie et société.* Ed. Jean Jacquot. Paris: Colloques Internationaux du Centre National de la Recherche Scientifique, 1968 525–76.

SPENCE, R. T. "The Cliffords, Earls of Cumberland, 1579–1646: A Study of Their Fortunes Based on Their Household and Estate Accounts." Diss. U of London, 1959.

SPIERS, W. L., ed. *The Notebook and Account Book of Nicholas Stone.* Oxford: Walpole Society, 1919.

SPINK, T. D. "Campion's Entertainment at Brougham Castle, 1617." *Music in English Renaissance Drama.* Ed. John Henderson Long. Lexington: U of Kentucky P, 1968.

STONE, LAWRENCE. "Companies of Players Entertained by the Earl of Cumberland and Lord Clifford, 1607–39." *Malone Society Collections* 5 (1960): 17–28.

SUCKLING, SIR JOHN. *The Works.* Ed. Thomas Clayton and Lester Albert Beaurline. Oxford: Clarendon, 1971.

WHINNEY, MARGARET. *Sculpture in Britain 1530 to 1830.* Harmondsworth: Penguin Books, 1964.

WHITAKER, THOMAS DUNHAM. *The History and Antiquities of the Deanery of Craven.* London, 1805.

WILLIAMSON, GEORGE CHARLES. *Lady Anne Clifford.* Kendal: T. Wilson, 1922.

WOOD, ANTHONY à *Athenae Oxonienses.* Ed. Philip Bliss. London, 1817.

WOODFILL, WALTER LINCOLN. *Musicians in English Society from Elizabeth to Charles I.* Princeton: Princeton UP, 1953.

WORP, JACOB ADOLPH. *Geschiedensis van den Amsterdamschen Schouwburg 1496–1772*. Amsterdam: S. L. van Looy, 1920.

WRIGHT, JOSEPH. *The English Dialect Dictionary*. Oxford, 1898.

Notes on Contributors

MARTIN BUTLER is a Lecturer in English at the University of Leeds. He has published a number of essays on early Stuart theater and *Theatre and Crisis 1632–1642* (1984).

ANTHONY J. CASCARDI is Associate Professor of Comparative Literature and Spanish at the University of California, Berkeley. He has recently published *The Bounds of Reason: Cervantes, Dostoevsky, Flaubert,* and is editor of the volume *Literature and the Question of Philosophy,* forthcoming from The Johns Hopkins University Press.

JONATHAN DOLLIMORE is Lecturer in the School of English and American Studies at the University of Sussex. He is the author of *Radical Tragedy* (1984) and co-editor, with Alan Sinfield, of *Political Shakespeare* (1985) and of a new series, Cultural Politics, being published by Manchester University Press. He is presently working on a book about sexuality, transgression, and subcultures.

RUTH EL SAFFAR, University Research Professor at the University of Illinois-Chicago, teaches Spanish literature of the Golden Age. Her most recent book, *Beyond Fiction: The Recovery of the Feminine in the Works of Cervantes* (1984), both culminates a series of studies on the fiction of Cervantes which she has carried out over the past eighteen years and points toward her current engagement with issues of gender and literary structure across the period 1500–1650.

GEORGE HUNTER, Professor of English at Yale University, is currently working on the English Drama 1585–1642 volume for the *Oxford History of English Literature.*

ANGUS MACKAY is Professor of History at the University of Edinburgh. His recent work has focused on ritual and violence: "Ritual and Propaganda in Fifteenth-Century Castile," *Past and Present* 107 (1985), and "The Hispanic Converso Predicament," *Transactions of the Royal Historical Society*, 5th series, 35 (1985).

GERALDINE MCKENDRICK, a Postgraduate Doctoral Research Scholar at the University of Edinburgh, has completed a thesis on the Franciscans in late medieval and early modern Castile. Of her published articles one in particular bridges the fields of history and literature: "The Danca de la Muerte of 1520 and Social Unrest in Seville," *Journal of Hispanic Philology* 3 (1979).

PHYLLIS RACKIN, Associate Professor of English at the University of Pennsylvania, has published articles and a book—*Shakespeare's Tragedies* (1978)—on Shakespeare's tragedies. She is currently completing a volume on his English history plays. Her most recent publications are "Anti-Historians: Women's Roles in Shakespeare's Histories," *Theatre Journal* 37 (1985), and "The Role of the Audience in Shakespeare's *Richard II*," *Shakespeare Quarterly* 36 (1985).